ENCYCLOPAEDIA OF EMINENT THINKERS

VOLUME-V: VINOBA

Encyclopaedia of Eminent Thinkers Series

Vol. I. The Political Thought of **Mahatma Gandhi**
Vol. II. The Political Thought of **Nehru**
Vol. III. The Political Thought of **Rabindra Nath Tagore**
Vol. IV. The Political Thought of **Radhakrishnan**
Vol. V. The Political Thought of **Vinoba**
Vol. VI. The Political Thought of **Aurobindo**
Vol. VII. The Political Thought of **Jayaprakash Narayan**
Vol. VIII. The Political Thought of **Vivekananda**
Vol. IX. The Political Thought of **Ambedkar**
Vol. X. The Political Thought of **M.N. Roy**

About the Author

K.S. Bharathi did his Master's Degree in Gandhian Thought, Peace-Science, Economics, and Political Science. He also did Postgraduate Diplomas in Politics, Public Administration, Population Dynamics, Gandhian Thought, Tourism, and Telgu. He has contributed some articles in learned journals. He is the author of : *Foundation of Gandhian Thought, Gandhi and Humanity, Socio-Religious Thoughts of Mahatma Gandhi, The Philosophy of Sarvodya, The Satyagraha of Mahatma Gandhi, Gandhi and Nehru, Foundations of Ambedkar Thought, The Social Philosophy of Mahatma Gandhi, Gandhian Approach to Rural Development, The Relevance of Gandhi, Gandhi and Vinoba, The Philosophical Foundations of Gandhian Thought, The Political Thought of Gandhi, The Economic Thought of Gandhi, The Social Thought of Gandhi,* and *The Quintessence and Chronology of Gandhi*. At present, he is the Head of the Postgraduate Department of Gandhian Thought of Nagpur University. He is the Chairman of the Board of Studies of Gandhian Thought, member of the Academic Council, member of the Faculty of Social Sciences, member of the Board of Examination, and member of the Doctoral Research Committee of Nagpur University.

ENCYCLOPAEDIA OF EMINENT THINKERS

VOLUME FIVE

THE POLITICAL THOUGHT OF VINOBA

K.S. BHARATHI
Head, P.G. Department of Gandhian Thought
Nagpur University, Nagpur

CONCEPT PUBLISHING COMPANY, NEW DELHI-110 059

ISBN 81-7022-689-9 (Vol. 5)

ISBN 81-7022-684-8 (Series)

First Published 1998

Published and Printed by
Ashok Kumar Mittal
Concept Publishing Company
A-15/16, Commercial Block, Mohan Garden
New Delhi-110059

Phones : 5649024, 5648039
Fax 091-011-5598898

TO
JOTHILAL

PREFACE

Vinoba had no concept of power of the state and power of economic resources. He could not convert his saintly appeal into political influence. He could not use his close contact with the rural people during 1951-66 to create any counter-force in Indian politics. On the contrary, he went to *maun* (silence) at every crucial point in the history of modern India. Further, he handed over the limited gains of his own movement to the political authority in India and after traversing 40,000 miles, he quietly retreated into his being.

In Vinoba the goal of life is to establish *Ram Raj*. It is a religious concept which involves social, political and economic involvement. The idealistic vision of creating a society fit for *Ram Raj* involves every member of society. Although an individual is important, it is the collective force which is deemed necessary. It is here that the relevance of many *dans* comes into focus.

The life and work of Vinoba have been discussed in the first chapter. Vinoba's ideas on Religion and Politics has been covered in the second chapter. His ideas on *Sarvodaya* has been analysed in the third chapter. His views on Third Power as such has been given in the fourth chapter. His ideas on *Swaraj Sastra* has been discussed in the last chapter.

I would like to place on record my indebtedness to scholars and thinkers whose ideas enabled me to bring out this book. I gratefully acknowledge the scholars from whose works I have drawn citations viz. Dr. Vishwanath Tandon, Dr. Suresh Ram, Dr. K. Shah, Prof. Vasant Nargolkar and Dr. Devendra Kumar. Besides I have made use of Vinoba's own writings and related literature. For these and all other, scholars who have thrown light on different ideas of Vinoba, I owe very much which I gratefully acknowledge.

So far as the writing of this book is concerned, whatever success I have achieved is due to relentless efforts, consistent help and encouragement of Dr. P.S.G. Kumar, Head, Department of Library and

Information Science, Nagpur University. I express my sincere gratitude to him.

I express my warm thanks to Mr. P.N. Hardas, and Mr. S.T. Patale of Nagpur University.

I am indebted to Mr. Ashok Kumar Mittal, Concept Publishing Company, New Delhi for publishing this book in such a short span of time. Finally I hold myself to blame for the errors and shortcomings, if any. This work would not have been completed without the grace of Lord Venkateswara of Tirumala and Alamelu Thayar of Trichanur.

K.S. BHARATHI

CONTENTS

1

LIFE AND WORK OF VINOBA

Vinoba's greatness both as an original thinker and as practitioner of his ideas was recognised by Gandhiji himself and therefore in 1940 he declared Vinoba as the first individual *satyagrahi*. Jayaprakash Narayan said, "Revolutionary and pathfinding thinkers in history have usually been followed by mere interpreters, systematisers, analysts. There have been rare exceptions, such as Rosa Luxemberg and Lenin in the case of Marx. Vinoba is such an exception in the case of Gandhi".[1]

Due to his discipleship and a close association with Gandhiji, the life and work of Vinoba has been inevitably linked with Gandhian thought. Vinoba himself never got tired of paying tribute of Gandhiji for shaping his life. However, a closer look at his thought reveals that he was an independent thinkers in his own right. While Gandhiji was concerned with the independence of India, Vinoba attempted to shape the destiny of post-independence India.

Vinoba was born on 11 September 1895 at Gagode. Gagode is a small village in the Pena Taluka of Colaba District of Maharashtra. The childhood of Vinoba was spent in this village up to the age of ten. He received his early education at home. His father Narhari was in Government service at Baroda. Shambhurao was his grandfather. He was deeply religious and devout, spending most of his time in *bhajan* and worship. Vinoba was greatly influenced by his grandfather. He had the golden opportunity of learning his first lessons in social reform and religious tolerance from his noble grandfather. Shambhurao's thinking was original and temperament liberal. On important festivals, he threw the temple open even to the *Harijans* of the town. Such an act on his part, doubtless required great courage in those days. He had offered a feast even to sweepers and chamars and himself served them with meals.

Shambhurao's wife, Gangabai, grandmother of Vinoba, was a very able and determined lady. She managed to learn reading and writing at the age of 55. She possessed a genial sense of humour and would face family troubles with courage and fortitude. Vinoba's father, Narhari was the eldest son. Rukminibai was his mother. They had five children. Vinoba was the eldest. His father was very scrupulous, methodical and disciplined in his behaviour. He was an admirer of western science and education and had the credit of producing the first *Khaki* cloth which was later used for the uniforms of the British soldiers. He obtained his Diploma from the Kala Bhavan in Baroda and worked for some time in the dyeing department of the Buckingham Mills. Later, he shifted to Baroda and served in the office of the Government as a senior typist-clerk. He observed strict punctuality in all his activities and possessed as keen sense of cleanliness. He was deeply interested in research and experiments in evolving a variety of colours for cloth-printing. He desired Vinoba to read English and French and proceed to foreign countries. He wrote several books on various aspects of Indian music.

Like Vinoba, his two brothers, Balkoba and Shivaji have remained *Brahmacharis* and devoted their lives to study and social service. Vinoba's early character was moulded mainly at the hands of his pious and affectionate mother. She led a life of simplicity, self-restraint and observed religious vows with regularity. She was so considerate to the so-called untouchables and always helped them in various ways. She encouraged Vinoba not to marry and remain a celebate throughout his life. She was so engrossed in singing devotional *bhajans*. She always asked her sons to shed fear of all kinds and harbour unfailing faith in *Ramanama*. She was a devotee of Lord Shiva. Vinoba used to read out the Marathi daily *Kesari* to his mother in order to keep her in touch with current events. She was keen to understand the *Gita* as well. She had a deep faith in the grace of God that she would invariably recite *Ramanama* while mixing leaven with milk for turning it into curds.

Vinoba was a voracious reader. But he read nothing that he did not digest and enjoy. He was also quite fond of newspapers. His father taught him English, Mathematics, etc., for three years. In 1910, he began regular school life as a student of the fourth English standard. In the beginning he fared very creditably in his class tests and examinations. He was fond of Mathematics. It is the exactness of mathematics which has become a part and parcel of his life. After passing his Matriculation in November 1913, he joined the Intermediate course. But he was not content with his life and ever since 1911 was thinking of leaving home for good and giving himself up to something higher.

Vinoba founded a Students' Society. This *Mandal* celebrated all festivals which fostered national consciousness. He was the central figure in this *Mandal*. His sharp intellect and forceful oratory had cast a spell over all. He makes people his own and so, once a person is attached to him in a bond of affection, the relationship stays for life. As an adolescent he was very hot-tempered and sarcastic. However, he was generally a happy-go-lucky person. He never paid any attention to his dress or haircut. He could easily walk five to seven miles at a stretch. On an average he used to walk about 15 miles a day.[2]

On 25 March 1916, Vinoba was on the train to Bombay with friends, for appearing the Intermediate examination. He got down at Surat and took the train for Varanasi. He stayed in Varanasi for 2-3 months. He stayed in a small room on the banks of Ganga, ate from an alms' centre. The whole day was for reading and contemplation. He followed the traditional method of studying Sanskrit through *Veda*, *Vedanga*. He used to attend debates. In Baroda, he had read Gandhiji's famous speech delivered on the Foundation day of Banares Hindu University. The vigorous speech of Gandhiji had deeply impressed him. Vinoba met Gandhiji for the first time in the Kocharab Ashram in Ahmedabad. Vinoba became an inmate of the Ashram.

To quote Vinoba, "Whether Gandhiji was subjecting me to his scrutiny, I know not. But according to me, I had tested him thoroughly and had I found him wanting, I could not have carried on with him. If he found, or would have later noticed, any number of deficiencies in me, he would still have kept me with himself. But as far as I am concerned, had I noticed any shortcoming or deficiency in his faith in Truth, I could not have stayed there at all".[3] In this way, the many-sided activities of Vinoba's *Sadhana* started. Meanwhile he felt the need for a year's change, for reasons of health as well as for further studies. He took a year's leave and went to Wai.

Vinoba returned to the *Ashram*, on the expiry of his one year's leave and joined the *Ashram* work. He did spinning, weaving, carding, etc. He used to enter deep into every job that he took up. A school was started in the *Ashram*. Vinoba was appointed to deliver religious discourses in this school. He taught Sanskrit and Mathematics. Gandhiji asked him to speak in the daily prayers on the *Gita*. Tilak attracted Vinoba from early age. He had very little direct contact with Tilak but the inner contact was deep and firm. His contribution to the Satyagraha Ashram was immensely important.

Gandhiji started a branch of the Satyagraha Ashram at Wardha.

He sent Vinoba with all the responsibilities for the Ashram. Vinoba conducted various experiments in Ashram life. He took the Ashram to be an experiment-oriented institution. He insisted on strict observance of self-discipline and demanded compliance with the Ashram rules. Once Gandhiji sent him to Vykom village in Travancore to guide a *Satyagraha.* He did it well. Under the leadership of Vinoba, such *Sadhana* went for two and a half to three decades. It covered experiments in various fields such as spinning, weaving, *nai talim*, cow-service, leper service, etc. Vinoba and his colleagues engaged themselves fervently to evolve the entire science and art of *Khadi. Nai Talim, Goseva, Kushta-seva* and other activities developed during this period and Vinoba trained devoted and life-long experts in each of these fields. He was laying great stress on self-restraint in Ashram life.

The Ashram atmosphere was constantly one of work as well of the trinity—*Bhakit, Jnan* and *Vairagua*. All work was done in the spirit of worship. In 1938, Vinoba had grown very weak due to hard labour and numerous experiments. Gandhiji asked him to look after his health and go for a change of climate. Vinoba decided to go and live in Pavanar. He spent his time in sereneness and happiness.

Vinoba linked *khadi* with the basic problem of rural unemployment. He set up a labour centre in Nalwadi, with a teacher. Whoever sought employment, could join the centre, learn spinning and earn his livelihood. Jamnalalji and others wanted that Vinoba's ideas should be placed before the people. The Ashram started a monthly *Maharashtra Dharma* edited by Vinoba, which later became a weekly. Efforts were made for the removal of untouchability. As a result, the Lakshminarayanan temple at Wardha was thrown open to *Harijans* as far back as 1928. In 1930, a campaign for prohibition yielded the result that 15 to 16 thousand toddy trees were cut off.

Totally Vinoba was arrested six times and served sentences for five and a half years in jail. He liked many aspects of jail life and said "real Ashram life can be lived and experienced only in jail. Counted clothes, a water-tumbler and a pot, these are all the utensils here. What else can go with the vow of non-accumulation. Timely bath, food, sleeping and walking. A very regular life. No freedom even to fall ill. The food is all along and every day tasteless. Do we observe more disciplines in the Ashram? We will have to introduce all these for improving Ashram life". His deep thinking, meditation and contemplation continued in the jail. Some valuable literature was created here. When he was in Nagpur jail, he wrote the *Swarajya-Shastra* and prepared an anthology of Marathi *bhajans* from Saint Jnaneswar, Eknath and Namdeo. From Seoni jail, he produced *Ishavasyavritti* and *Sthitaprajna-darshan.* In the last jail term, he was pondering over the idea of 'release from all institutions', i.e. serving all institutions without being bound up with any. He also wanted to identify himself with those who lived on manual labour.

When Vinoba left home, he had a desire to go to Himalayas, and also keenness to go to Bengal. Apparently he reached neither; but Vinoba says: "Mentally, I reached both simultaneously. In Gandhiji I found the tranquillity of Himalayas and also the revolutionary fervour of Bengal. The line of thinking I got there was a unique combination of both Revolution and Absolute Tranquillity. I got much from Gandhiji's Ashram; as a consequence, I experienced that life is identical and integrated. After entering the Ashram, I could perceive this; I got my eyes as it were. Gandhiji's Ashram is my alma mater which gave me this insight"[4] Regarding Vinoba, Gandhiji says, "He is one of the rare jewels of the Ashram. He has come to purify the Ashram with his own religious merit; he has come not to receive but to give".[5]

After Gandhiji's assassination two or three years passed in the search for the path. In March 1948, there was a conference of the country's constructive workers at Sewagram. It was mainly due to Vinoba's inspiration that the Sarvodaya Samaj and later Sarva Seva Sangh, were started. At Jawaharlal's request, he agreed to spend six months, on an experimental basis, in helping the rehabilitation of the destitudes. He went Delhi. He worked hard to rehabilitate persons belonging to the Mewa tribe from Delhi, Punjab and Rajasthan.

Vinoba spread the message of love and goodwill in the atmosphere of communal narrow-mindedness. His truthfulness, spirit of devotion and deep study of all religions wielded a tremendous influence. He was invited by the Muslims to accompany them to the *Dargah-Shareef* and offer prayers. There he offered the common inter-religious prayer. He travelled to other places in the country and tried to create a climate of communal harmony and equal respect for all religions.

After about 21 months of nation-wide travels, Vinoba returned to the Ashram. In the meantime, he had seen that even though the country had attained political independence, Gandhiji's chief mission was still incomplete. The incomplete work of Gandhiji was to be advanced mainly through freedom from economic exploitation and freedom from political bondage. Vinoba started a vigorous campaign for freedom from wealth. All commodities required for living, should be produced by manual labour in the Ashram itself, to the extent possible. This was a unique experiment of labour-based living.

The Sarvodaya conference was to be held at Shivarampalli in Andhra Pradesh. Vinoba agreed to attend it at the insistence of his friends. He started his journey on foot from Sevagram on 7 March 1951. In thirty days, he walked about 300 miles to reach the place. In the presence of all the constructive workers, he said, "the mission to be achieved after independence is very profound indeed and also difficult. The task is to function as foundation stones of society. We have to take up now the work of social and economical revolution". For every worker, he profounded a five-point programme—inner purification, external cleanliness, manual labour, tranquillity and dedication. At the end of the conference, he announced that he would like to see for himself the conditions in Telangana through a journey on foot. He started his journey on 15 April. He visited communist prisoners in the jail at Hyderabad. He talked to them with deep sympathy.

On 18 April 1951, Vinoba reached Pochampalli on foot. He went round the village. The Harijans in the village asked him for help. He went into deep thought, as he could not see any way out. Mr. Ramachandra Reddy came forward to donate 100 acres of land. Vinoba was overwhelmed. In this way *Bhoodan* was started. That night, he could not sleep for three to four hours. He went on asking, and people went on giving. On 27 June, he returned to Pavanar. Till then, 12,000 acres of land were received in *Bhoodan* in 70 days. In Pavanar, he got busy with the experiment on the programme for freedom from wealth. He had no idea of going out again soon thereafter.

Jawaharlal Nehru invited Vinoba to come to Delhi and have detailed discussions with himself and with the Planning Commission. Vinoba accepted the invitation and decided to undertake a *padayatra*. He stayed in Delhi for 10 days. He had detailed discussion with Nehru as also with the Planning Commission. He almost challenged the Planning Commission. He said, "If, besides heavy industries, you have any other programmes which could provide work to everyone in the country. I would set fire to *charkha* and not shed a tear. But I am sure that without the help of *charkha* and the village industries, you cannot provide work to the entire population of India. You accept the target that employment should be provided to everyone, but do not accept the responsibility to plan for reaching the target. So I have to say that your planning is not for the entire country but for merely a certain section of it".[6] He had presented the essential outlines of planning according to Gandhian way of thinking. His thinking was absolutely clear.

From Kanyakumari to Kashmir, thousands and lakhs of acres of land were received in donation. Land, for which people ruin themselves in litigation or commit murders and blood-shed, was offered by people, with love. Thousands donated lakhs of acres for distribution to their own landless brothers. In all 42 lakh acres of land was received and 15 lakhs were actually distributed. His march continued and reached new dimensions. From land-gifts came the idea of *Gramdan* (village-gift) in Mangroth in Uttar Pradesh. The Mangroth people offered the entire land in their village to him. From such an incident, the idea of village-gift arose. The village-gift idea gave a new direction to the *Bhoodan* movement.

In 1953, there was a Sarvodaya conference at Chandil. At Chandil, Vinoba declared, "We have to generate people's strength and arouse it, as opposed to the power of violence and different from the power of Government. Violence, in fact, will not be of use. Our work is to create conditions in the country in which there is no occasion to apply the sanction of law, which we have entrusted to the Government. This people's power is not opposed to the power of law but is different from it. All our work should be geared towards ultimately bringing about the condition of non-dependence on governmental authority for punishment".[7]

During his Bengal tours in 1963, Vinoba put forth the idea of *gramdan* as a comprehensive programme of village self-rule. The ownership of land was to vest in the village society, as in the original concept. The second step of *gramdan* was to lay down the rule that the land-holders in these villages were to donate 1/20 of their holding for the landless. The third matter about *gramdan* was that while everyone will produce or earn something on his land, he will give 1/40 of it annually to the village society. Non-cultivators will give their one day's earnings every month. Labourers will offer their labour for a day every month. In this manner, *gramdan* become an efficient and well-planned programme of Village *swarajya*. It achieved a coordination of individual freedom and dedication to society, a perfect balancing of freedom and equality. He explained time and again that a village-family cannot be constituted until *gramdan* is obtained. Without it there is no solid foundation for our comprehensive work.

Along with *gramdan*, Vinoba suggested several other programmes necessary for building up a Sarvodaya society. He continued to lay emphasis on the *Shantisena* programme. He used to speak of taking *khadi* production programme to the villages and said that *khadi* was directly linked with economic independence as well as with village self-rule. To quote Jayaprakash Narayan, "After Gandhiji, if any single name in the entire world has given a ray of hope, it is that of Vinoba. His activities like *Bhoodan, Gramdan* and *Shantisena* have drawn the attention of the whole world. With programmes like *Bhoodan*, he has started a stupendous effort to introduce spiritual values in collective social life. The most important index of the development of a society is the development of its human qualities. Vinoba's programmes offer a solution to the problem of building up a new society, on the basis of ethical values. Vinoba's movement is a great experiment of human development as well as of social reconstruction. That is why the entire world looks up to him."[8]

Vinoba had an idea firmly fixed in his mind, that *Sarvodaya* cannot be brought about if we become only a Naradmuni. He was also sure that one could not bring about a change in government's attitude just somehow. The Bihar campaign was nothing but a stupendous effort to secure people's consent for *Sarvodaya* idea. In the Rajgir conference, Vinoba declared many matters relating to the future line of work. He said, "So far we were after this programme with a single-mindedness, which some would regard a defect. Now we have completed one stage. So we should add a few more matters. We must start work in cities also mainly for two or three purposes. We have to liberate municipalities from party-politics; that should not enter there. Next, we have to organise each *mohalla* as a *Shantisena* centre. For raising a *Shantisena* for the whole city, a well-thought out plan will have to be prepared. Thirdly, we have to explain to the labour class not to associate their trade unions with any party. Otherwise, their interests tend to get neglected and political interests achieve their own purpose. Moreover, special efforts should be made to draw labour towards *Sarvodaya* ideology. Fourthly, in cities it would not be enough if the millionaires and industrialists give a little in donation. We should try that they accept their full social responsibility. We should put up such a demand, and should develop such strength that the demands are not ignored or refused".[9]

From 1951 onwards, for about 25 years, there was an experiment on country-wide scale for introducing Gandhian ideology in the socio-economic field. It was proved that land could be obtained by compassion instead by bloodshed or by force of law. In 1963, Vinoba said, "I had formerly thought that after donating his land, the donar had no further right to interfere in its distribution. This was a grave mistake. It occurred due to false pride of bringing about a revolution and presumption of virtuous merit in doing so. Instead if it had been then decided that the donor could himself distribute his land, much more land would have been promptly distributed and a bond of love would have developed between donor and donee".[10]

To quote E.F. Schumacher, "The future of India, I believe, will be decided, not in Delhi or Caluctta, nor in Bombay or Madras. But in her 500,000 villages and small towns. That is where 85 per cent of her population live. The most devoted, self-sacrificing and successful, original work may have been done in a particular village, the kind of work from which millions of villages of the world over would benefit and the chances are that nobody outside that village ever hears about it or, if someone happens to hear of if, that he has no effective means of obtaining the information to enable him to do likewise. How welcome, therefore, to have book about India which deals with the real India, a straight forward report of what I have seen and what I have heard. It presents Fragments of vision, and the vision is one of rural reconstruction, rural regeneration through *gramdan. Gramdan* is a path of change without violence, a revolution of non-violence. I hope and trust that Mrs. Linton's most informative and realistic report on her travels through rural India will help to open people's eyes to the urgent need for a systematic organisation and communication of the kind of knowledge without which no change in the spiritual, ethical and social order can become effective economically".[11]

The word *bhoodan* was born in 1951 and the *gramdan* idea occurred in 1952. Its new form was put before the public in 1963. A glimpse of its potentiality to become extensive was seen by 1969. The thought and feeling agitated the public at large. A philosophy of *Sarvodaya* took shape and it became clearer that *Hind Swaraj* would be meaningful only in *Gram-swaraj*. While Vinoba was in the Ashram, solitary *Sadhana*, profound experiments and silent service were the main features. He remained permanently attached to the freedom movement and the various constructive programmes. He watched all the events in the country, including political ones. He thought that evading social problems did not give peace to the mind.

The idea of national integration became a strong reality to Vinoba. National integration can be visualised only when (1) the entire population could be aroused by a common sentiment, (2) when they could feel the vibrations of common experience simultaneously, and (3) when they could revere a number of great men reflecting the entire nation in themselves. Vinoba delivered about 20,000 talks in the *yatra*. His speech flowed ceaselessly like the Ganga.

Once Pandit Nehru said, "On the one hand, we have the five-year plan, agricultural improvement and the beginning of various industries; on the other, the stir of activities of social reforms and social welfare, the heat of political and economic, differences of opinion and of disputes regarding language and boundaries, in addition, disruptive tendencies, the aspirations for national unity and the unhappy incidents tending towards despair and discord. In brief, on the stage of modern India, so full of complexities and yet forging ahead, Vinoba's feeble form stands up with the strength of the back-bone. He is humble and mild. Even so, he represents the strength of India's hoary past and his eyes shine with the lustre of our unseen future. He embodies the soul and the tradition of India, and of Gandhiji, more than anyone else".[12]

After independence Vinoba put before all the workers the new goal of *Sarvodaya*. He initiated them to *Sarvodaya* ideology. He made them personally give up their selfish attitudes and think in terms of social good. He drew them to purer and nobler joy and cultivated their entire approach to life in his own inimitable way. He trained all his workers to be all-India servants. He was deliberately trying to educate these workers to develop their independent thinking also. He laid stress on meditation and studies.

In 1960, during March, a sacred event took place. Twenty-one dacoits came and surrendered themselves, as if violence was surrendering its arms before non-violence. Vinoba handed over to the Police the dacoits who had surrendered. He travelled in Kashmir. On entering Kashmir he said, "God willing, I wish to do three things—to see, to hear and to love. I wish to apply here all the power of love, which God has given me. If I am found wanting, I will ask for more strength from Him. If I have to speak, I will speak only for this and will not speak more".[13] In Kashmir, he wandered a lot, mixing freely with the common men. He went into deep and remote villages where few outsiders reach. There also he met people in their homes and enquired about their difficulties.

In September 1962, Vinoba had his journey on foot for 16 days in East Pakistan. He used to hold silent prayers there, as he often did in India in very large gatherings. In 1962, our borders had to face Chinese aggression. He was then touring in the interior of Bengal. His attitude provided correct guidance to the country in the troubled times of Chinese aggression. His non-violence is discriminating in many ways, such as discrimination between justice and injustice, discriminating about our limitations of the development of *ahimsa*, discrimination of not opposing traditional measures for achieving what *ahimsa* cannot at present achieve and discrimination to apply oneself wholly to strengthening the power of *ahimsa*.

Vinoba started a movement to remove obscene posters. His remarks on unbecoming posters are absolutely logical. He said, "I am not against cinema, I advocate scientific progress. I desire that we should have good films and I am not raising a cry against even bad ones as yet. To stop that would require public opinion. A demand for better censorship could also be raised. While people pay for seeing films in a cinema house, the posters are displayed on public roads, they naturally occur to every one. Sometimes they are so ugly that a good person cannot even bear their sight. Thus, this constitutes an aggression on public liberty. They leave a very bad impression on tender minds, for children they provide free and compulsory education on sex-indulgence. What is obscene may be decided by a committee of known and reputed citizens. For sisters, it becomes a programme to protect their modesty".[14]

In 1965, there was a holocaust in the country on the question of language. The entire country was agitated, but there was a violent storm in the South. The Prime Minister and the Chief Ministers of all States accepted Vinoba's Three-Point Formula—there should be no violence; Hindi should not be imposed on those who want English to stay; English should not be imposed on those who want Hindi.

Vinoba always stressed purity of heart and discard of ego. When a person is completely egoless and when he is completely dedicated, his action, thought and meditation draw limitless strength. He has reached a firm conviction that narrow-mindedness cannot solve the problems confronting humanity—problems of language, religious sects, national boundaries, commerce and trade, exploitation and so on—all very often problems of our attachment to the body. They are based on narrow-mindedness.

In October 1970, Vinoba said that he had received an inner direction for confining himself to Pavanar. Naturally he gave up all other fields of work. He observed silence for a year from December 1974. On 25 December 1976, he announced complete freedom from all activity. He relinquished responsibility for the direct work of the movement. He said that he would no longer go to the people, but will offer advice to those who come to him naturally. In short, he went on reducing external activity as far as possible so that the distraction from the special experience of entering the abstract may be gradually minimised.

On 7 June 1970, Vinoba moved to Brahmavidya Mandir. Now he had given up direct activity in society, but was not opposed to social contacts. Through his abstract meditation and *abhidhyan*, he was advising and guiding people who came to him, and thus he was trying to keep his activities to the minimum possible. Adding *Nagari* Script and *Brahma Vidya* to the existing programmes of *Gramdan*, *Shantisena* and *Acharya Kula*, he gave to the workers a five-point programme. He said that for carrying out this programme we have to secure the cooperation of five powers.

Regarding the cooperation of five powers Vinoba said, "These five powers are like our five fingers. The first is the thumb, which is sturdy; it stands for people's power. It has to stand on the strength of *ahimsa* and *satya*. The second one is the small finger the inner urge which stands for the power of good men. In simple words, it is the power of the *sevaks*, workers engaged in life-long service on the basis of moral principles like truth, while themselves living on the strength of these principles. The third finger is index finger which points to the correct way; this stands for the power of scholars. The scholars have to guide all, while keeping themselves aloof; they study the events in the world disinterestedly and place their opinion before the world. The fourth is the power of the rich i.e. those engaged in business and industries—big and small. They also constitute a power, before whom Gandhiji placed the concept of trusteeship. This is the middle finger. The fifth finger is called the nameless one, *anamika*. People wear their rings in it and call it ring-finger as it has no particular work assigned to it. It has only to bring about coordination between all the powers; it stands for government power. Today it may have assumed supremacy but some day its importance will certainly diminish and it will remain a power in name only—cooperation of all these powers will have to be secured by those who work in public."[15]

In April 1974, with regard to Bihar unrest, Vinoba said, "Corruption, inflation, unemployment, and educational changes—the planks on which the agitation has started—are all matters requiring consideration, not agitation. Who does not agree that there should be reforms in education? What can you get by agitating about it? What is required is careful consideration. Inflation is a question of money-economy, if we want to get rid of it, we have to attain as much freedom from markets as possible. It will not to do say that Government alone is responsible for inflation. It may be feasible to set up a commission to examine the changes required in the election laws or in the Constitution. Moreover, there is the question of setting up candidates from rural areas. Corruption that prevails in other spheres is of many forms. How can you remove it by agitating? And if you just agitate for removing government, it will ultimately be an opposition of democracy itself".[16]

What Vinoba wanted to say was that today the world has become so small that even the politics of this country should be viewed in the context of the world situation. The consequences of each step should be correctly weighed. The main problem now-a-days is that the country is breaking up. Therefore, we should work as a cementing factor. Otherwise, the country's unity will be in danger. Our country is surrounded by dictatorial neighbours. If the Central Government falls in such circumstances it may not be able to recover. If any such situation arises there are numerous countries, big and small, waiting for the opportunity to benefit from it. Indiraji's foreign policy is firm and wise. She may have committed many serious blunders in internal matters. This also raises many important questions indeed. But attempt should be made to solve all of them through negotiation. This will maintain a climate of cooperation and goodwill in the country. Our role should be to bring people together, not to disrupt them. Jayaprakash Narayan wanted to say that corruption and misuse of authority were rampant to such an extent in the administration and government machinery that citizens have lost all faith in the government.

On 26 June 1975, National Emergency was proclaimed. Jayaprakash Narayan and others were sent to jail. Vinoba was observing silence during the period. His first reaction was that the Emergency was an outcome of the churning going on in the country for a year or two. He imagined that it will be used only as an *ad hoc* shock treatment. But later the real situation unfolded itself to him gradually and the true nature of Emergency also became clearer. In the form of a maxim, he had mentioned in July that this was an occasion for discipline and once or twice, he had also expounded its implications which however were not made public. Therefore, the maxim was much misused by government and led to a good deal of undeserved misunderstanding about Vinoba. His clear exposition became public only much later on 25 December when his one year's silence ended.

To quote Vinoba, "The *acharyas* lay down the dictates of discipline—States lay down the dictates of the government. We should understand well the difference between the role of *acharyas* and of the State. If the world remains only under the rule of the State, there could be no rest: if it is guided by the dictates of the *acharyas*, there will be peace in the world. Who are the *acharyas*? I have described in the words of Guru Nanak that an *acharya* is one who is fearless non-partisan and without any animosity. He never loses his peace of mind; he is never perturbed. If people behave according to the guidance of *acharyas*, it will be good for all. This is discipline—the discipline of the *acharyas*. If Government opposes their dictates, there could be an occasion for *satyagraha* against it. I trust our Government will do nothing, contradictory to the *acharyas*' dictates. Hence, in India there will be no occasion for *satyagraha*".[17]

In 1976, Vinoba had announced his fast to begin on 11 September, if cow-slaughter was not banned in the entire country. Government applied the censor's whip and did not allow even this decision to be published. Vinoba remarked, "What cowards have we become? Our press would not publish such a pious resolution because of government censorship. Supposing tomorrow I pass away during the fast and Government declares that Vinoba died of heart-failure, will you all publish it that way? Government can arrest and bind you, even send you to jail. It can do nothing more. But if you have courage, they cannot harm you. God helps those who help themselves. Everyone should fearlessly go to the temple and say what one considers correct and proper. Not moving underground but openly, you must place before people your views and thoughts, whether about the Emergency or about cow-slaughter. How many would they keep in jail"?[18] After this, Government had a talk with him and announced that all the States would legislate about ban on cow-slaughter within a year or so.

During Emergency Vinoba was pondering a lot. He was searching for some non-violent panacea to solve the problem and create an atmosphere of mutual trust and good-will in the country. He wanted that while all win no one loses; just as when India gained independence, the British gained the goodwill of Indians because they left without any rancour. But Vinoba found no such panacea nor did he get any inner direction. After the Emergency, the Sarva Seva Sangh met. He advised that the Sangh may be wound up. This however, did not happen, but his affection for the Sangh remained undiminished. He said that there were many good persons in the Sangh. Whenever his advice was sought, he gave it lovingly. His love for Jayaprakash Narayan continued as before. There was no change in their mutual relations; they were unaffected by the differences.

At the age of 84, Vinoba undertook a fast for securing a ban on cow-slaughter. After five days of fast, the Central Government announced that legislation in the light of the Supreme Court's decision will be taken up; necessary amendments in the Constitution will be made to put this subject on the Concurrent List. Vinoba said, "From a universal point of view, man should not exploit nature. Indian culture accepted the fact that man is also an indivisible part of nature, and as a consequence of experiments spread over thousands of years, included the cow and its progeny as family members of the human race. It is fine example of the mutual relationship of animal and man. In the Indian economy the cow has the highest place; it is the pivot of rural economy. Only agriculture and animal husbandry have the potentiality to feed the sixty crores of our people. Indian agriculture is based on the bullock. Cow-dung gives the best compost and *Gobar*-gas plant is the best source of energy".[19]

Vinoba tried to find the dynamics of social change through non-violence and love. Never before was a serious effort directed towards this until Gandhiji's constructive programme made such an attempt. He carried out a large scale experiment on it. He says that *satyagraha* is used now-a-days mainly for securing relief from the oppression of laws. But it is not an instrument of revolution. There is a place for *satyagraha* even in democracy, because *satyagraha* is a way of life and a way of conduct. At the same time in special situations it may also be a remedy.

Vinoba has expounded public morality in great detail. He has given some practical hints for immediate action and also some thoughts to bring about basic alterations. Unfortunately no one paid heed to him when he was spelling out a code of public morality, and pointing out some particular danger-spots in democracy as adopted by us from the West. There are some fine instances of his sarcasm. He said, "In the field of thought, you have more often to refute the theories of those nearer to you than of those more remote. Sharkaracharya did not refute the atheists so much as he refuted *Sankhyavada*, which is closer to his theory. That is because what is close to us differs from us only in some small detail. Thus there is greater probability of being misled. So the closest ideas have to be formulated and defended first. Later, it does become quite clear as to where the real point of difference is. When we turn to social work, the position is reversed. If you oppose the near ones in this, it would amount to driving them away. One has to keep this line of demarcation between social service and spiritual thought".[20]

Swarajya for Gandhiji and *Gramswarajya* for Vinoba were not political objectives, but spiritual goals. Their concepts of *swarajya* are very much the same. Vinoba took the vow of celibacy and social service at the age of ten. Ever since, his mind has been fastened to one equation: *Swa-rajya*—our own kingdom—the kingdom of the soul. Years later, he wrote *Swarajya-Shashtra. Rajya* is one thing, *Swarajya* is quite another. You can get kingdom by violence. *Swarajya* is impossible without non-violence. Hence a thoughtful person will not desire a kingdom, but he pines for *Swarajya. Swarajya* will mean everyman's kingdom i.e. a kingdom which everyone regards as his own, in other words the kingdom of all, or *Ramrajya.* He says in the *Samya-Sutra,* "you get freedom from government, when you realise your own soul-power".

Vinoba did not die a natural death. He invited it. If one carefully reads the various accounts, later made available of his extraordinary decision and behaviour in the first fortnight of November 1982, one would not fail to notice that the idea of giving up voluntarily 'the Holy Ghost' probably first occurred to him on 7 November. It is difficult to say whether he had, before this, thought of discarding the age-worn and disease-ridden body specifically by abstaining from taking both food and water. Vinoba did not believed in dying of a disease. He wanted to die of starvation as a result of a deliberate decision. He died a very peaceful death on the morning of 15 November.

Mr. Rajiv Gandhi paid a visit to Vinoba on 15 September 1982, exactly two months before the latter's self-invited death. Vinoba said to Rajiv, Your name is Rajiv. If we remove *Ra* from your name, what remains is *jiva.* Now if we add *daya* to *jiva,* we get the word *jivadaya* which means 'compassion to all living beings'. 'You must show compassion to all living things'.[21] Vinoba wanted Mr. Rajiv Gandhi to appreciate his earnest plea for legal and constitutional protection to all cows and bullocks, irrespective of their age, utility or condition of health, and also convey once more to his mother Vinoba's expectations from her as Prime Minister.

Vinoba was a rationalist. But he believed that there are subjects where Reason cannot take us far and we have to accept things on faith. Faith then does not contradict Reason, but transcends it. Faith in God was thus the cornerstone of Vinoba's philosophy of life. For years, he meditated deeply on the mysteries of nature and the mystery that is man. He had also studied the mystic experiences of various saints and sages, of prophets and religious preachers, of seers and servants, as recorded in the scriptures of the prominent religions of the world.

REFERENCES

1. Vishwanath Tandon. *The Social and Political Philosophy of Sarvodaya after Gandhi*, p. 3.
2. Kanti Shah. *Vinoba Life and Mission*. pp. 4-6.
3. *Ibid.*, p. 17.
4. *Ibid.*, p. 32.
5. *Ibid.*
6. *Ibid.*, p. 49.
7. *Ibid.*, pp. 53-54.
8. *Ibid.*, p. 62.
9. *Ibid.*, pp. 67-68.
10. *Ibid.*, pp. 70-71.
11. *Ibid.*, p. 74.
12. *Ibid.*, p. 83.
13. *Ibid.*, p. 88.
14. *Ibid.*, p. 95.
15. *Ibid.*, pp. 113-114.
16. *Ibid.*, pp. 116-117.
17. *Ibid.*, p. 125.
18. *Ibid.*, p. 127.
19. *Ibid.*, p. 134.
20. *Ibid.*, pp. 145-146.
21. *Maitri*, October 1982, p. 883.

2

ON RELIGION AND POLITICS

Vinoba was a spiritualist who drew his inspiration from the diverse religious traditions of the world. In understanding his thought, one has to be careful of the use of the word 'religion'. He defined the boundaries of religion as understood conventionally in terms of certain beliefs and practices. He was more concerned with the process that made a person religious rather than with the observance of rules. It was he who declared that the age of religion and politics was over and the age of science and spirituality had dawned. This statement reflects his sentiments for a new humanity and a fresh outlook on life.

Vinoba was a religious thinker. A marked characteristic of his spiritual thinking is its synthetic nature. He was a product of Hindu culture from which he inherited the tradition of religious tolerance. He exercised a rigorous spiritual discipline and advocated the same for others. It is this discipline which became the backbone of his religious experiences. His thought and actions are directly connected with his conception of God. His conception of the Divine can be characterised as polymorphic monism. He followed the *Upanishadic* dictum which states that reality is one but the sages speak of it in many ways. Thus he could relate himself to all religions equally as testified by his writings on different faiths. Based on his conception of a Universal God, he attacked the narrow interpretations of God by various religions. He looked at God as a concrete reality rather than as an abstract force. He believed in a universal ethical basis. He lived the life of a *bhakta*, steeped in his love for God, and performed his service for the lowliest of people in the spirit of detached action. He saw God in the poor, the lowly, and the have-nots of society.[1]

Vinoba called for the unity among all religions. This concern for 'religious universalism' was heightened by his awareness that India was a land of religions. He disliked the fact that on the basis of religion Indian society was divided. He felt that religions were more like denominations which preached dogmas, perpetuating religious exclusivism. He said, "The *Quran* teaches us; *Allah-hu-wahid*, meaning God is one. We have been taught it all along. Now we would have to add: Man is one—*Insan-hu-wahid*. Whereas old spirituality stresses the unity of God, the new spirituality stresses the unity of man".[2]

Vinoba proclaimed that an individual was a universal person and therefore needed a universal religion. With a universal vision he proclaimed *satyagraha* against those temples that refused entry to the Harijans. He contended that in today's scientific age, the religions would have to go. He did not imply the end of religion but rather the birth of a new spiritual religion. He felt that this new religion was gradually being born. Therefore he called for an extended meaning of the word *Vedanta* which means the end of the *Vedas*. He pointed out that as the word suggested the end of the *Vedas*, there should be an end of the orthodoxy based on the *Vedas*.[3]

Vinoba emphasised the uniqueness of each religion and drew from the resources of different scriptures. He affirmed that collectively all religions gave testimony to one single truth. And under this universal truth all religions should unite. For synthesis of religions, he advocated three things. First, study of the words of religions in order to reconcile them. Second, experience of different religions. Third, to put into practice the teachings of religions for a better living.[4] He encouraged people of different faiths to worship together. What he put into practice was what he identified as four basic elements of a universal religion, e.g., faith, love, truth and sacrifice. From the *Gita* he received the message of *karmayoga*, and perhaps from Western religions he received the direction to apply actions in the service of God and humanity.

Vinoba idealised Ramakrishna who lived the life of a Christian, a Muslim, and a Hindu. Like Ramakrishna, Vinoba also tried to synthesise the spirituality of world religions. He felt that a communion within world's great religions was possible, but it entailed practising of the perennial truth that they all believed in. In his life, one finds a synthesis of the values of many religions. As a Hindu, he emulated the life of a *sanyasin* by following all four *yogas* according to their respective traditions. He drew his inspiration from the teachings of Hinduism on self-control and self-search. As a Christian, his life reflects the influence of beatitudes as found in the teachings of Jesus. A sense of humility, lessening of pride, love for peace, and service for others are clearly manifest in his life. As a Buddhist, he showed the path of a *Bodhisattva*. Like Buddha, he took his message to the people on foot. He also received inspiration from Mahavira. He admitted that he had the mental bent of Mahavira.[5]

Vinoba's saintly character was nurtured by a sense of freedom from dogma that can come only through religious experiences. It was his religious maturity that allowed him to see good in other people and value in their opinions. His love for God and humanity is clearly manifested in the sacrifices he made throughout his life. For the love of God, he left his home at an early age. And, for the love of humanity, he joined Gandhiji's movement. His love for both God and humanity found an expression in his struggle to establish a *Sarvodaya* society. He often spoke of Jesus who taught to love one's enemies, and proved it through the example of his own life. He believed that the message of the Christ would be practised soon and science would help to do it.[6] His attitude of love was informed by the religious heritage of mankind.

Vinoba considers the purpose of life as search for truth. To him, God is an aspect of Brahman, looked at from the human point of view. God is immanent but not limited by mere co-extension with the cosmos. We can see God anywhere and everywhere in nature as much in the inanimate things as in the animate. God is the universal soul and resides in the hearts of all creatures. He said, "If anyone believes in the goodness of man, I shall be satisfied. Belief in human goodness is the beginning of belief in God. Therefore if one believes in the essential goodness of man, he will be on the right path. This will naturally deepen his experience and he may reach the stage of realising God".[7] Belief in God is not a matter of blind faith.

God is inferential Brahman in contrast to the soul which itself is Brahman. Vinoba said, "If there is something in the body, a similar thing is also in the universe. If there is blood in the body, there is water outside. If there is breath in the body, there is air outside. Since there is the sun outside, there are eyes inside. There is consciousness outside and so there is also consciousness inside".[8] He equates God with Brahman which is not new.

Belief in God is not a matter of blind faith. Vinoba said, "Some sociologists have arrived at the conclusion that the idea of God is a criterion of the unscientific terror-stricken mind of the primitive man. They hold that as the light of science will spread, this darkness present in the form of belief in God will also disappear. Had God really been darkness, His disappearance would both have been necessary and beneficial. The God of those is surely in danger who have conceived. Him as different from he soul, as the Creator of the universe and as one who resides in some corner outside the world in the seventh or forty-ninth heaven. But such is not the conception of God taught to us by the *Vedanta.* The Supreme is the purest form of soul and devotion to God is the acme of self-efforts".[9]

Mystics are able to see God with their eyes. Men of God all over the world testify to this fact. Universal brotherhood will not be established in the world unless the paternal authority of God is accepted. If anyone believes in the goodness of man, Vinoba will be satisfied. Belief in human goodness is the beginning of belief in God. Therefore if one believes in the essential goodness of man, he will be on the right path. This will naturally deepen his experience and he may reach the stage of realising God.

According to Vinoba, an atheist is he who does not believe that good actions produce good results; and bad actions, bad results. A theist is one who believes in the theory of *karma,* even though he has no faith in God. None becomes religious by invoking the name of religion, and nor does he become a devotee by taking the name of God. One who lacks integrity in life, non-violence in conduct, religiousness in dealings, cannot be a theist. A sincere atheist is nearer to God than a nominal theist. More atheism has been spread by conflicts among theists than by atheists themselves. Atheism is not a new phenomenon. It is as old as faith in God. There is no room to hold that atheism is more prevalent these days.

Exploitation of our fellow-men means disrespect to God. If we harbour pride and consider ourselves in some way superior to others, that too implies disrespect to God. Devotion must express itself in our day-to-day life. Compassion, love and sympathy are the outer expressions of devotion. A person who has real devotion will see the image of God that resides in every human heart. The highest way of devotion is surely shedding all narrow personal self-interest. The one characteristic of the devotee is that he reduces himself to zero and believes that whatever exists around him is the manifestation of God who is perfect. The devotee shall always bear in mind that all men and women who live around him are so many forms of his Master and he is their servant. This is true service, true surrender as the servant to the Master, and indeed this is true devotion".[10]

God is truth, all good, fearless and devoid of animosity. If we worship God but do not develop His qualities, we should consider our worship to have been in vain. The form of worship of God has changed. Those who would not realise it, would be doing wrong things in the name of devotion. We continue to worship with flowers and fruits but without genuine devotion. God is to be sought in our hearts. He can be worshipped only with flowers of real devotion and the fruits of an incessant quest of true knowledge.

Regarding various forms of worship, Vinoba said, "God has innumerable attributes. A devotee worships Him as one endowed with the particular quality he finds himself lacking in. Different religions differ from each other since they have developed in different regions. However, they all aim at worshipping God. He has innumerable forms, and may even be said to be formless. Of these innumerable forms, some prefer one and some prefer others. This variety in worship removes the monotony of life. Just as several melodies go to make music complete, similarly the various forms of worship make the devotion complete".[11]

Prayer is an effort of a living being to remember God gratefully. In spite of the fact that the various religions, all built up by the services and sacrifices of many great men, have some major or minor differences in their doctrines and observations, there is no difference of opinion in any religion on this matter that prayer performed collectively or individually, by repetitions of His name or in some other way, is indispensable both for the individual as well as society, for his or its life, moral uplift, purification of mind, search for truth and maintenance of mental equilibrium in the sorrows and attachments of life.

Regarding the functions of prayer, Vinoba said, "Prayer is the last act of our daily routine. During working hours we do many acts of commissions and omissions. At the end of the day, we stand before Him and say: Merciful and Omniscient Lord! Thou knowest everything, even without our expressing them in so many words. But we feel a consolation in speaking about Thee in our language. So we pray, let us not take credit and feel proud of whatever good acts we have performed. Save us from pride and give us the wisdom to do acts without egotism. We might also have committed wrongs, some knowingly and others unknowingly. Forgive us all these failings. By forgiveness we do not mean that we should escape from the punishments for such acts. Do punish us, for Thy punishment itself is forgiveness. But have favour on us and guard us against committing such sins. If we open our hearts before Him in this way, we would experience as if a wondrous beam of light entered our heart and illuminated and strengthened our being. There is no source of energy in the world which, if we draw from it, does not decrease, except the one emanating from God, who is within us".[12]

Vinoba compares prayer to a bath, food and sleep. It has the virtues of all the three. Sleep gives rest and replenishes energy. Prayer also provides rest and imparts spiritual strength to man. While food nourishes the physical body, prayer does the same to the mind and heart. A bath cleanses this body, while the prayer purifies the mind and heart. Thus what all these three do together for the physical body, prayer does for the mind and heart.

Regarding genuine prayer, Vinoba said, "Prayer is no mechanical activity. It is not simply performed by words of mouth. It involves the practice of passing the whole day in the light of the spirit of the words of the prayer, impressing one's heart with it. All of us describe God reverently in our own ways but it has not been said that a particular description is His best or complete description. God is still satisfied with it just as a father is satisfied with the inarticulate expressions of his tiny child. Even so, silent prayer is accepted as one of the best forms of prayer. If children and parents sit together in silent prayer, it is a good practice and elevates society. The habit of science will be conducive to peace and non-violence. Silence expresses the feeling for God more than words ever can. Everyone can contemplate on the God of his conception when he is silent. It is only in silence that one can experience God in the recesses of one's heart. In silence, one's intellect is submerged in the feeling for God. Both individual and collective prayer have utility in their respective fields. Collective prayer is necessary for social consciousness. Unison of voice strengthens the feeling of unity. At the same time, individual prayer should not be given up".[13]

Man is not simply an animal. The predominating quality of an animal is vitality, *prana*. It is not so with man. The word *manusya*, (man), stands for one who contemplate, who thinks. In the case of animals their capacity is limited. But it is not so with man. Man differs from an animal in that he is not satisfied merely with meeting the demands of the body. There is the urge in him to get rid of social bonds and to identify himself with the whole world. This is the thirst of the soul. In case the two are satisfied together, there would be peace and amity in society. God has bestowed three gifts on man—speech, organs of actions and a sympathetic heart. A man can measure his development by the extent he has been able to control his mind and heart and his mind has calmed down. The original state of the soul is that of calmness. Hence real progress will be presumed to lie in the attainment of the utmost tranquillity.

A man has both good and evil desires, but, on the whole, it is the good desires that prove more powerful and it is they which bring him satisfaction. A man's heart, we must understand, is always good at the core. It may get rusted outside due to various external factors; its internal goodness remains always the same, whatever the outward appearance. By nature, man is noble. That is why he pays respect to righteous persons and not to thieves and dacoits. Man is forced to act wrongly by the force of circumstances. He is carried away by the currents. But the moment he would realise it, he would change at once on one plea or another. One good point about those who are really wicked is that they have great faith in God. They are quite near to those who are really virtuous, like the two ends of a circle. That makes their conversion quite easy. People might have become devoid of morality, but they have not acquired love for immortality. They love truth and morality. The present lust for money is due to the existing economic structure being based on it. It the social order be such that people get work and their needs are satisfied, selfish people will be turned into good people.

The supreme ideal of a man's life is *mukti* (liberation). The attainment of happiness is not the purpose of life, for it is a quality of the soul itself. None can survive without joy, no matter whether less or more of it. The real purpose is self-realisation. Liberation consists in ridding oneself of the narrow personal ego and in merging oneself in the larger self of the society. *Moksha* is liberation from attachment, anger, lust, illusion, ignorance, etc. If these perversions have been got rid of, *moksha* has been attained.

Regarding the happiness, Vinoba said "The fulfilment of being born as a human being does not lie in the enjoyment of physical pleasures, but in making others happy, no matter how little it be. A life full of service is life. The rest of it is only a form of death. But if the service is not selfless, it does not remain service. Happiness does not mean the pleasure of the heart or mind. Pleasure has little to do with happiness. Happiness is abiding, pleasure is transient. Many people today are suffering mentally and emotionally for the sake of their country. They find happiness in such suffering. This is because suffering is sometimes salutary, as it is when accompanied by a sense of benignant service. True happiness is to be found in peace, not ir a disturbed or agitated consciousness. Its source is tranquillity of spirit. We feel happy only when we are overpowered by the feeling of oneness".[14]

Desire, anger and greed are the three great enemies of an aspirant. Greed is the most universal and subtle among them. In reality, the enemy is not outside but inside. Our indolence, desire for indulgence, mutual quarrels, ego preventing unity between us, ignorance, these are the enemies, and they appear externally assuming the form of outsiders. Hence our first task is to destroy the inner enemies, and then the external ones would disappear without efforts. A righteous man does not die. As long as he is alive, he is confined to only one physical body. If a godly man leaves the body and he has no desire left, he lives in the world through many bodies, and it is what is termed liberation.

An important idea in Hinduism is that of rebirth. According to it, if a person is not able to complete the work he is doing in any particular birth, he tries to complete it in the next. Thus he goes on evolving. After once being born as a human being, one would, later on, either get human birth or some higher one. However, if some desire of his is so strong that it could only be satisfied as an animal, he would get that birth and would even relish it. It is a mistake to think that one is born rich or poor in accordance with his deeds in the previous birth being good or bad. Good deeds of the past birth result in good thoughts and freedom from egotism, while evil actions give rise to evil desires and to proclivity for wrong deeds. An individual soul has its own regular chain of *sanskaras* (tendencies), and he is born of particular parents accordingly. His own regular chain constitutes one line and a second one is constituted of family tendencies. The individual soul is born at the point of their intersection.

Regarding the law of *karma*, Vinoba said, "We shall certainly reap in the next birth the consequences of the actions of the present one. But some good and bad deeds are so intense that their fruits are experienced in this very life. The Indian people have some wrong conceptions. They think that pleasures and pains experienced by us are the fruits of actions of the previous births. Hence everyone must put up with one's fate. This is a mistaken idea. No doubt, everyone has his own destiny. Yet, some part of it is common. We are born in the same village because of it. Thus what comes to be destined does not pertain to an individual alone. The law of *karma* is not to penalise you. The award of punishment is an indication of God's love. He wishes to reform you. There is something over and above justice, and it is Mercy. We must reap the consequences of our evil, deeds, but if God takes mercy on us, we can be exempted from them. No matter how wicked one is, if he is repentant he becomes a good man".[15]

Man has enough freedom to carve out his future. He has been given a free hand to decide what he would like to become in his next birth. God will not impose His will on us in this matter. If you want to continue whirling in the cycle of life and death, He will ordain it. Or if you want to move closer to God with the hope of merging in Him one day, it is also possible. We get the physical body in accordance with the previous birth, but as soon as we have been born, the effects of our previous life are over. After that it depends on ourselves how we would act. This would determine our next birth. What is termed as 'fate' are the efforts of yesterday and the efforts of today would determine the fate of tomorrow.

A religion deals with several matters. One is 'worship' involving direct relationship with God, the second is 'ethics' concerned with truth, non-violence, etc. The third are 'customs' and 'practices' which pertain to various rites performed at death, birth, etc. The fourth is mythology, stories, etc. Thus a religion has several components. The more we concentrate on the fundamental oneness of humanity the more do the different religions appear as enriching and strengthening one another. Vinoba regards the different religions as merely different forms of worship. Each form has its distinctive merit. When the different ways meet together all these merits gather together and make a rich and full pattern. The ethical principles are the same in all religions. All religions lead to God. They are life different roads; one seems to go to the east, another to the west, but still everyone leading to and terminating in God.

Organisation and religion are contradiction in terms. Due to organisation, religion has not become that force it would otherwise have become. Surely, the progress would have been slow, yet the condition would have been far better than what it is today. There are many who pride in the name of religion, but there are few who practise the essence of religion. Religion and love must flow freely within a society. We like to keep our God in a distant heaven. We are afraid to bring Him down to the earth.

Regarding science and religion, Vinoba said, "The subject matters of science and religion are different. The situation is similar to that of eyes and ears between whom there is no opposition because they have their independent fields. Some hold that science is opposed to religion. They feel that religion would die because of science. But I think otherwise. Up to now there was no science and consequently, really speaking, religion had not come into existence. Now as science would advance, pure religion would come to be enunciated. Because of science only true religion would survive and not the false one. Only a religion which is rational, which is not a figment of imagination, which has arisen above desires and has done away with all sorts of distinctions including that of worship, would be able to survive".[16]

Karmayoga does not mean becoming less spiritual in attitude. It would not only result in fruits equal to those of *Dhyanayoga* but in something more. In the path of action one is expected to utilise to the maximum this earthly sheath—this physical body with all its powers for promoting good. All the organs of work and the senses of perception including the mind and the intellect, etc., have to be employed methodically with a view to purifying them in course of time. Action is as fuel to knowledge. In order to keep the sacrificial fire of knowledge constantly burning, one must supply the fuel in the form of action. The essence of the matter is that the *Karmayogi*, by surrendering the desire for fruit, receives an infinite reward. His life proceeds evenly. He is radiant in body and mind. The society in which he moves is happy. He attains inward purity and also *jnana*. And society being rid of hypocrisy and deceit, the ideal of a perfect life comes within our reach. This, experience shows, is the greatness of a *karmayogi*.

Both the *sannyasi* and *karmayogi* are *jnanis*, seers, and are entitled to the same high throne. Though the names are different, the substance is the same. They are two modes of the same reality. A wheel in rapid motion seems at rest. The state of the *sannyasi* is similar. From his *shanti*, his peace and steadiness, flows infinite power, endless movement. Though all the endeavours of the *sannyasi* have ceased, and come to a rest, he does mighty deeds. To do nothing, and yet to do all things, is possible for the *siddha*, the perfected one, not for the *sadhak*, the seeker. *Karmayoga* is both the way and the goal, but *sannyas* is only goal. From the point of view of the *sadhak, karmayoga* is preferable to *sannyasa*.

One should utter the name of God, use one's hands in doing God's work and see Him inside his own self. When all these three go on together, the path of devotion is accomplished in all its aspects. In the path of devotion, remembering the name of god has been glorified. *Nirguna* and *saguna* complement each other, they are not incompatible. Starting from *saguna*, one has to tread the path to the goal of *nirguna*; *nirguna* too needs the water of *saguna* to cleanse the subtle impurities of the mind. Each gains lustre from the other.

There are three important things in *dhyanayoga* (the *yoga* of meditation), namely (1) one-pointedness of mind, (2) setting bound to one's life, to help to achieve this, and (3) a state of equanimity or evenness of vision. One-pointedness of mind means controlling its movements. Setting bound to one's life means doing actions after weighing and measuring them. Evenness of vision means having the nobility to think in terms of the whole world. These three together make up *dhyanayoga*. To achieve these three, one needs the help of practice and detachment.

Spirituality is that science which enables you to perceive and recognise the whole infinite universe in your own self. It is impossible to comprehend fully the true nature of the universe and to find out who is its creator, for the universe is macrocosmic as well as microcosmic. And yet an effort can be made to comprehend its nature. This effort can be made through observation which could be either outward or inward. Physics helps to understand the outward aspects of the universe, while metaphysics enables us to comprehend a little the inner nature of the universe. It is, however, not possible to attain to integral knowledge through the pursuit of physical sciences. To try to know who is the Creator and to realise Him is again more difficult. That is why the only easy way of knowing and realising Him is to try to find Him in the individual self. This itself is known as spirituality.

It is wrong to separate spiritual progress and material advance. If the two are conceived separately, both will remain incomplete. It cannot be said that materially backward countries are spiritually advanced, while it is equally fallacious to think that materially developed countries like America are spiritually poor. Where there is only apparent material abundance, decay will be discernible; and where the emphasis is one-sidedly on spiritual progress, there too life will be lopsided. Thus progress can only be all-sided.

In Vinoba's vocabulary, the word 'spiritual' has a deeper significance and must not be confused with traditional religion. Whenever scientists met Vinoba, he always expressed his faith in the everwidening horizon of science and its beneficial effect on human growth. He compared science to the engine of the automobile and spirituality to its steering wheel. He used to say that the two can work only together and that one is incomplete without the other. He said, "The science has made many new discoveries and recently has found out the power of the Atom. Similarly the spirituality also will have to produce a power like that residing in the atom. In the realm of spirituality also there is an atom which is smaller than the smallest and that it resides in the human heart. It is small no doubt but the smaller it is the greater is its power of explosion. In earlier, times the experiments of spirituality were limited to one's own family and like science were experienced. But now as science has become universal and world wide. Spirituality too must keep pace with it. Essentially spirituality is universal but its application was done in a family, where people worked together and shared and sacrificed for each other. This in a way was the expression of the universal spirituality on the micro level of the family. Now the time has come that this spirituality confined to the family is widened on the worldwide scale".[17]

In a speech at Pattamundai on 1 March 1955, Vinoba said, "Science has two kinds of power—one is the power to destroy and the other to construct. Science can thus serve the humanity and also destroy it. When man discovered the use of fire, he could cook his food on it as well as burn his house. But whether to use the discovery of fire to burn the houses or cook food was not decided by science but by spirituality. As a bird flies on two wings, similarly man is endowed with two powers of spirituality and science. Both of these he has to use in unison. In a motor car there is a mechanism for giving it speed and another mechanism to give it direction. Whether the speed is of 10 miles, 20 miles, 30 miles and for this there is an accelerator. And what direction a motor car is to take—whether to east, west, or south, for that there is another instrument. Both these instruments are essential for the car to move. But if either one of these is absent you cannot use the car. With our eyes we cannot move, we can only see the direction. The spirituality is like eyes; and science is like our feet. Without spirituality we will be blind. Similarly even if a person has eyes but no feet to move then where can he go. Hence without science, this world cannot work and without spirituality no proper direction can be given to science".[18]

Religion and spirituality are two different things. Religion is the outer form of the philosophical attitude that is propagated by a certain school of thought. The spirit of all religions is a quest to understand the unity in diversity and simplicity in complexity. The basic tenets of all religious teachers are much the same and to give expression to them in our day-to-day life the religious practices vary due to social, cultural, geographical, and other environmental factors. As the spirit of all religions is one, the spirituality behind all religions is the same.

Vinoba therefore says that religions have tended to divide man and man. Wars have been fought in the name of religion. As time passes, the outer form of religions will fade away and the inner spirit will remain. As the rational logical reasoning guides man to understand the religions, the real spirit of the divine will reign supreme. It is in this vain that Vinoba believes that politics will go and science will remain. Religions will give place to spirituality and politics to science. Here politics divides and science unites. Both science and spirituality are the cohesive powers and if humanity is to develop, the two must reinforce each other.

When the goal of life is self-realisation and the means for reaching the goal is both devotion and service, it is natural that ethics should find an important place in such as scheme of life. It is a matter of course, therefore, that Vinoba emphasises ethics as an essential part of his philosophy of life. Wisdom of the ages, in fact, finds expression through him when he speaks on ethical problems. Yet his views on morality appear fresh and original, because his utterances come directly from the depths of his soul. Ethics is the science of what is morally right and what is morally wrong.

A law of *dharma*, morality to be true must be applicable to all. Any such rule which is applicable to some and not to others, is no *dharma* at all. To speak truth, to love all mankind, to be compassionate, all these rules are applicable to all. Vinoba does not differentiate between moral and spiritual planes. Spiritual plane is higher, but the moral plane is not lower. It is nearer humanity. One is the ladder, the other, the destination. It is not possible for a man to be a spiritual being without first being a moral being. It is our duty to act in a manner conducive to a proper functioning of the creation, society and the physical body. We build up many good or bad institutions, but these three are no creation of ours. Hence it is our inherent duty to make good the harm done to these three institutions through *yajna*, *dana* and *tapa*. A right action is one that gives us peace of mind; an unrighteous action is that which deprives us of it.

Regarding *Svadharma*, Vinoba said, "*Svadharma* implies that every person has his own independent duties. It vary from individual to individual. But since a man is also a part of society, we may say that everyone should render service to society. However, each has his own special qualities and he should serve society by developing them well. The *svadharma* of the *Gita* is so comprehensive that it is applicable to all. To determine one's *svadharma*, one should consider what is helpful and appropriate to one's nature and situation, and what duty falls to one. Different individuals may have different *svadharma*. The *svadharma* of an individual may also vary from time to time. The *dharma* of an individual person varies according to the times and the development of his inclinations. The *Gita* teaches that the *svadharma* of an individual consists of his duties at a particular time. When a man is born, his *svadharma* too is born with him. As a child has no need to go in search of his mother, no one need go in search of *svadharma*. It is ours, right from the beginning".[19]

Dharma has two aspects, one changeless and the other changing. The observance of truth is as much a duty today as it was in days gone by, and as much in other countries as in India. The difference of time and space does not limit it. It is of the kind of eternal varieties, which are the same always. So are love and compassion. But the rules of conduct through which they are sought to be expressed cannot last for all the time. They change according to age and circumstances and country. Devotion is again an eternal *dharma* and equally true for all, but form and ceremonial designed to express it will differ. What we must do therefore is to hold fast to this changeless soul of *dharma* and keep it continually on our mind.

The number of the observances can be less or more and its does not vary, but non-violence, truth and some others are eternal. The vows have the capacity of protecting men and society. As a result of their observance, an individual like Gandhiji became a Mahatma. They embody the quintessence of the lives of all saints. They are not only meant for a recluse. They are for him and for the whole society. It is said these days that 'vows' constitute a bondage, but it is a misleading idea. The vows do not give trouble. They form a good straight path. When the road is good, we do not worry. Vows imply treading a straight path. They make it easy, they make men free.

The world is sustained by truth. It subsists because there is more truth in the world than untruth. If untruth acquires predominance over truth, the world would come to an end. There is no inherent strength in untruth. Even for its existence, it has necessarily to depend upon truth. Four means have been suggested for the realisation of self. The first among them is truth, and it is very important. If we put all the moral philosophy of the world on one side and truth on the other, the latter would outweigh. Truth is the highest principle of morality, while all others are secondary to its. Truth is that which makes us realise the existence of conscience and brings satisfaction to it. When the conscience does not feel satisfied or is shocked, there is untruth. That is, the conscience is a witness to truth and untruth. Truth cannot be defined. It is self-evident. As a matter of fact man is essentially truthful by nature. Truth is more natural than untruth. We see this in children. Gandhiji said that truth could be attained by non-violence. Vinoba's idea is that truth can be attained by humility, objectivity and non-insistence. It is so in science. There is no dogmatism in it. Only that is considered as correct which is testified by experiment. Truth and beauty are not opposed to each other.

Non-violence does not mean 'not to commit violence'. Its one meaning is to be fearless, the second is to cooperate lovingly, and the third is to have faith in constructive work. It is not merely an external activity. It is an inner faith. It is the name for the maintenance of balance in thinking and not allowing the equanimity of mind to be disturbed. It is that which keeps different persons together and which tries to seek non-difference in differences, while violence is that which creates divisions and increases differences. A life on non-violence means not merely occasional sacrifice but perpetual sacrifice, not merely sacrifice but joy in sacrifice. Non-attachment and universal love are necessary if we wish to practise non-violence. Truth without non-violence would not be truth, and non-violence devoid of truth would not be non-violence. The strength of non-violence lies in the balance in thinking, gentleness in words and restraint in actions. Impatience does not help in the growth of non-violence. There is no dearth of weapons in the armoury of non-violence. It can never fail. Non-violence has such capacity that even if the whole world is drowning, a single individual can save himself by swimming. The power of non-violence does not depend upon number, but on inner purity. There is no conflict between non-violence and legislation. A non-violent movement prepares the minds of the people, and if a legislation is enacted in accordance with it, it comes within non-violence. The characteristic of non-violence is that everyone has full freedom and yet everyone follows voluntarily all rules and regulations. Non-violence needs discipline and planning much more than violence. It does not mean lenient tolerance; nor does it mean intolerable vigorous restraint.

Science has two aspects, the pure and the applied. Non-violence also has two aspects, the theoretical and the practical. Vinoba said, "I hold that only pure non-violence is conducive to happiness, but when it is a matter of practising it several questions arise. Some say on the basis of the *Bible* that it need not be looked into as to what party has been in the wrong, who committed the aggression, what was the former situation, history, etc. All that one has to do is to ask one's own and other countries to stop violence. Despite all my sympathy for them, it has not been possible for me to adopt that position. Moreover, the question also arises whether non-violence is an attitude of mind or an external technique, and the reply is that it is not only a technique but an attitude as well. And since the attitude is the main element, I am not yet clear that in case an occasion arises for external resistance and from the viewpoint of society it appears unavoidable, even then it should be avoided".[20]

Brahmacharya means that a man directs the path of his life to the search for *Brahman*. It is a positive concept. It does not merely mean that we have to avoid any particular thing, but there is something tangible, positive, to be done. It means the greatest aim of all, achieving the realisation of the Lord. In *Brahmacharya* it is important to lead the senses and the mind into the right direction. If we think in terms of suppressing them, our evolution will be hindered. Therefore, all the senses should be rightly used. They should be correctly restrained; this will be very helpful to aspirants. As long as the vow of *brahmacharya* is not observed, the observance of the vows of truth and non-violence is well-nigh impossible. The reading of sacred books, and the company of saintly men, is certainly a great help towards a life of *brahmacharya*. But to live a natural life in the open air, and to work bare bodied in the sunlight, is an even greater help. It is a wrong idea that a *brahmachari* should avoid coming in contact with women. It leads to the imposition of unnecessary artificial restrictions. If a *brahmachari* feels that he should not look at any woman who may have come before him, we should regard that as his shortcoming. *Brahmacharya* imparts greater acuteness to intelligence. Today, world population is increasing rapidly and the available land is decreasing. Therefore people are saying that we should have small families. This means that *brahmacharya* now has a new social context.

The observance of *brahmacharya* is found difficult because we are not able to control our palate. An important measure of success in that spiritual endeavour is the degree of victory over palate. That is why control of the palate is reckoned as a vow, and, in accordance with it, an aspirant should take care that his diet becomes purer and cleaner. Food is only a means to maintain the physical body. It should not be accorded greater importance. If we are slave to the palate, we consume more than the need. This makes society to suffer. One fond of tasty food is a slave and he undermines his strength. If we overeat, our sexual passion is excited. Consequently, we do harm to society. For true service, purity in food in necessary. As is the food so is the mind. The food we eat should be regulated. Not what food we take, but how much we take, is the more important question. It does matter what food we choose to eat, but it matters even more that it is in right measure.

Non-stealing does not merely mean taking a thing not given by others, but also accepting something without giving anything to others. Consumption without sacrifice is theft. It is theft to use foodgrains, cloth and other things without directly participating in their production.

Non-possession is a name for 'liberality', though people understand it differently. They hold that non-possession stands for poverty. But it is not so. In fact it means that no sooner there is accumulation, it is to be passed on to another. Where wealth flows, it is non-possession. The true meaning of *aparigraha* is to discard the sense of identity with one's body. For, the body itself is the main thing among one's accumulation. There is no external measurement for non-possession. Vinoba holds that one may even be observing it though living in great splendour. Hence there can be no external measurement. Let everyone find answer within himself. When a man deals in the world, he comes to acquire possessions, however less. Hence the way to be free of that sin is to surrender a part of it to society. When non-possession comes to be recognised as the basic principle of social order, there will be minimum need of power to coerce for the government to rule. There are five features of a non-possessive society, namely, (1) there will be an abundance of wealth, (2) the wealth will be equally distributed among the members of the society, (3) there will be no accumulation of such rubbish as liquor and cigarettes, (4) there will be accumulation of certain things on priority basis, the order being foodgrains, cloth, housing, agriculturai implements, means of knowledge, means of recreation and so on, and (5) there will be minimum accumulation of money.

The vow of non-stealing regulates the mode of acquiring wealth, while the vow of non-possession regulates the quantity. In consequence, both are one and the same. Non-stealing and non-possession supplement each other in making economic dealings moral, without which *dharma* cannot be established in individual and social life. Truth and non-violence are basic, but in the economic field they can only find expression in non-stealing and non-possession. Economic matters play a very big role in life and the science of morality cannot be indifferent to it. On the contrary. It is the responsibility of ethics to regulate and control it. In the *Shastras*, non-possession is considered as a necessary concomitant of non-stealing. If theft is regarded as a crime, accumulation of property and inequality also must be regarded as sinful, whereas at present one is punished and the other is praised.

Bread labour should be done as a worship. It should be a daily rule with us not to take food without doing some physical labour. Vinoba will not give food to anyone, be he even a professor or a judge, unless he has worked for two to four hours. Non-violence cannot be attained without physical labour. Today bodily labour commands no prestige in society. The peasant works hard but he likes to see his son on some job in an office. Bread labour alone is a mode prescribed by nature for man to earn his living. An observance of this vow makes the observance of others easy. If one gets bored by physical labour, it is a sign of degeneration. The *varna* system does not mean that some should be absolutely exempt from physical labour. It only means that everyone should contribute his share to the society in accordance with his capacities. It is wrong to say that some may do only physical labour while others do only mental labour. God has created us with brains, hands and also hunger. If He had desired that only a few persons should produce things and others should do only intellectual work, He would have given only brains to some and only hands to others, for He is Omnipotent. But He has not done so. He has given hunger to all and so also hands. It is, therefore, against His will that some persons do only intellectual work like reading, writing, etc., and the rest merely do the physical labour of production.

Fearlessness represents a state of mind which can be brought about only by a change in the way of man's thinking. It can only be derived from the inner self. If one has the inner strength to die rather than to live with indignity, a child even can face any danger fearlessly. Fear and morality are naturally contradictory. A disposition to fearlessness is the basis of divine virtues. If one leads a virtuous life in constant fear of temptations, death would lose its dreadfulness. Fearlessness is of three kinds—fearlessness based on knowledge, fearlessness based on God and fearlessness based on discernment. Fearlessness based on knowledge is that fearlessness which results from the knowledge of dangers and the irremedies. The fearlessness based on God, makes one fully fearless. But it cannot be acquired without prolonged efforts, devotion and continued practice. Fearlessness based on discernment restraints one from needless and reckless daring, and if one has no option but to face a danger, it makes him do so keeping his mind calm out of discernment.

Swadeshi means self-reliance in a comprehensive sense. It is an inherent duty of man. Just as non-violence is an established rule of *dharma*, similarly *swadeshi* is a rule of conduct. Things nearer to us, be it the neighbours, prevailing customs or morality, are inherited by us, and therefore are dear to us. In this lies the secret of *swadeshi*. If we boycott articles giving an extreme interpretation to the moral duty of *swadeshi*, we shall prove ourselves to be men of a long past world. We shall be antiquated. It is not that *swadeshi* forbids dealings with outsiders. There is good scope in it for reciprocal dealings. But it is wrong to burden others with work we can well do ourselves. In short, the plan should be one which will make each village a self-sufficient unit with regard to food, cloth, education, etc.

The idea of having equal feelings for all religions also implies the acknowledgement that one's own religion is imperfect. If we are imperfect, the religions conceived by us are also imperfect. All religions are partial embodiments of truth. The various religions should be understood as different forms of worship. Vinoba was of the opinion that there are four essential ingredients of *Sarva-Dharma-Samabhava*, the feeling of equality for all religions. One of them is faith in one's own religion; the second is respect for all religions; the third is the reformation of one's religion; and the fourth one, which naturally follows from the three, is opposition to irreligiousness. When all these four ingredients are found together, there is *Sarva-Dharma-Samabhava*.

The task of eradicating untouchability has got to be done in two ways: (1) By improving the economic condition and mentality of the *Harijans*, and (2) By purifying the Hindu religion. Vinoba coined the word *sparsha-bhavana* (the feeling of touchability). This word is comprehensive. The feeling should be that we should have touch with the whole world.

In addition to the above eleven vows, Vinoba introduced one more vow, namely *Anida* which means not to speak ill of others. We should only talk of the good qualities of a man in his absence. If we have to point out his shortcomings, it should be done to him in private or in the presence of friends before whom it would not be improper to do so. If we hear something praiseworthy about someone, we should be inclined to agree with it immediately. If we hear something evil, our heart and mind should not be prone to accept it. We should not look upon anybody with suspicion. It acts as a great obstacle in the way of devotion and service.[21]

Self-government means ruling over oneself. It follows that we shall have *Swaraj* when all people have acquired the strength of self-control and have realised their duties. Until then we have only government. It is one mark of *Swaraj* not to allow any outside power in the world to exercise control over oneself. And the second mark of *Swaraj* is not to exercise power over any other. These two things together make *Swaraj*—no submission and no exploitation. Under *Swaraj* the smallest child will have the strength to stand against the whole society to declare its resolve not to suffer injustice. The society in which even a person who lacks physical strength stands firmly to express his independent opinion against the whole of it for the protection of morality, is free. Every adult person, whether great or small, has now one vote for himself. But conferring the right of vote in itself does not mean *Swaraj*. *Swaraj* will come into being when all are valued equally, all are honoured equally and all are socially held equal. But *Swaraj* of this kind does not exist in any country of the world.

The Self-government has two aspects. One is of the decentralised power, i.e., the whole power be distributed among the villages and the affairs of a village should be conducted by the villagers themselves. The second is of giving such education, inculcating such psychology and teaching such philosophy as are in consonance with a belief in the power of love and non-violence as against that in the power of violence. We must devote ourselves to building up an independent people's power, and that in itself will be our true service both to the government and to the nation. Vinoba said, "By an independent people's power I mean a power inheriting in the people, which is totally opposed to the power of violence, but is other than the power of the law, and which it must be our tasks to call into being. We have handed over the power of the law to our government, and although it contains an element of coercion, we regard it as being in a different class from out and out violence because society as a whole has conferred these legal powers on the government. It is our task to create a situation in the country in which there will be no need to use even these sanctions of the law. If we can do that we shall have fulfilled our own true dharma".[22]

The State exists merely to apply to the whole society the economic principle which is found everywhere to a greater or less extent in the family. This is the task beyond the power of the family. If the state does not do this service, there is no need for its existence. If instead of performing this service it produces economic inequality it will be right to destroy it and to establish anarchy. Administrators have spread fear of anarchy everywhere in order to make people submit meekly to their rule, however, bad it may be.

Three different theories of government are before us. The first is that the state will ultimately wither away and be transformed into a stateless system; but, in order to bring it about, we must in the present exercise the maximum power. The second theory is that some form of government has always existed in the past, exists now, and will continue to exist in the future; a society without a government is a sheer impossibility. Therefore society must be so ordered as to ensure the welfare of all. There may be certain amount of decentralisation, but all important matters must be under the centre. The third is our own theory. We too believe in a stateless society as our ultimate goal. We recognise that in the preliminary stages a certain measure of government is necessary, but we do not agree that it will continue to be necessary at a later stage. Neither do we agree that totalitarian dictatorship is necessary to ensure progress towards a stateless society. On the contrary we propose to proceed by decentralising administration and authority. In the final stage there would be no coercion but a purely moral authority, said Vinoba.

Government is not something natural, it is man-made. But the condition today is such that the moment, one is born, he comes under the control of a government. The chief cause of all the turmoil and unrest found in the world is the managerial class. Some managers are rulers, some are officers, some are policemen, and soldiers, and some are lawyers and judges. Thus they are of different types. There are some religious managers known as priests. The world is in disorder because of these managers. The people are like a well, while the government is like a bucket. In other words. the power of the people is greater.

'Power politics' is one thing and 'strength politics' another. Some people run after power politics, but power results in the erosion of strength. Strength is increased by selfless service. Political power does not confer the strength needed to increase our social welfare. That strength and that spirit can only be found in those who serve society with single-minded devotion, untrammelled by bonds or by the duties of any office. Therefore there should be within a society a large group continually engaged in service and continually on the alert. It should have experience in public affairs, but it should hold no position of authority and it should express itself fearlessly and dispassionately on public issues, so as to exert a moral influence both on the government and on the people. Such a group can be effective only if it keeps clear of office, not contemptuously but with an understanding of the limitation of power and with the realisation that the source of strength lies not in power but in the service of the community.

For hundreds of years there had been foreign rule. The people were made inactive. Everything is done by government servants. A mentality has developed that we have to do nothing. We want the same thing to continue after independence. It is termed 'freedom' when we are completely slaves. There is inactivity in the nature of India. We have to remove it and then work. Only then India will progress. At present entering politics only means lack of involvement in the service of the people. Involvement in politics implies involvement in jealousy, hatred, quarrels and in attempts to serve one's own interests. Nothing is being done for the good of others. In a country like India where there are innumerable differences such as those of language, religion, caste, etc., politics will only create further differences. Hence, there can be no progress in India without ending politics and establishing *lokniti*—politics of the people. Vinoba wants to say that this is an age of science. In this age, politics has been left with no strength now. Man has acquired new types of weapons. Hence. if divisive politics will prosper, man is sure to be annihilated.

A real democracy means that every citizen is responsible for the welfare of society, and that every citizen's talents are being developed and used. Real democracy must rest itself not on force of arms but on the power of *ahimsa* and the organised good-will of the people. That is the democracy we are striving for. The difference between democracy and other polities is that democrats do not believe in army. In their philosophy army has a secondary place. However, the recognition given to the army in practice though not wishing it in theory, converts democracy into military rule. Hence it should only be based on non-violence.

Our modern democracy came into being as a protest against the power of kings, and for that reason it suffers from the same faults as the monarchy it displaced —the real power remains in the hands of a Central Government. Vinoba said, "Democracy is like a dairy milk, while monarchy is like a single cow's milk. A democratic government is representative of the sum total of its people's development".[23] Mere counting of heads and elections are not the essence of democracy. At present we are talking about democracy and at the same time keeping capitalist economy and a military regime. We give lip-service to democracy but our actions are anti-democratic. That is why our democracy bears so little fruit and may soon bear none at all. The present democracy is a slave of bureaucracy.

It is no use saying that in a democracy people have the right and the opportunity to change the government every five years. A little serious thought will show how hollow this contention is. Four or five years are not a small period in these days when scientific advance has changed all the old values of time and space. What one government does today in the five years of its tenure very often binds the successive governments also, and cannot be undone or left unfinished by them. Vinoba said, "Democracy and military rule are very close. For democracy claims to work for the welfare of society through representatives. Society is not asked to work for its own . . . and we would set everything right, make society happy and abolish disparities. But when they are unable to fulfil their promises, people get dissatisfied. At the same time, they also feel oppressed by the laws. Under such conditions it becomes easy for the army to assume power, assuring the people of comforts and ease".[24]

The democracy adopted in our country is a senseless imitation of the West. Here conditions are not like those prevalent there. Hence a lot of problems, troubles and obstacles have arisen. So long as we do not evolve and adopt a democracy that suits the conditions of our country, our troubles will not end. We shall have to seek measures that avoid conflicts and differences within the country. In India a democratic set-up has to be built up, consistent with the peculiar conditions and circumstances of the country. We have forgotten major languages and an equal number of states. The country is a vast one, about five times in area and six times to seven times in population compared to England. In our country we have a number of religions with rich and philosophical backgrounds. The difference is easily perceptible, and yet we try to fully imitate England.

Vinoba emphasised on two points. First, in elections the individual rather than the party should be given preference. Elections to *Gram Panchayats*, municipal boards, etc., should be free of party lines. Members of the Lok Sabha should be regarded not as representatives of parties but of the whole country. Secondly, he wants the formation of an association or society which should be absolutely immune to party bickerings and affiliations. Such an association would have equal consideration for all parties and serve them equally. It will work as a lubricant to prevent clashes between them. If these two conditions are fulfilled, we shall achieve some success in democracy in India.

Lokniti replaces the word *rajniti*. Though the word is new, the idea is an old one. It means that the authority should be that of love and it should be exercised from within. There should be no external authority. *Lokniti* means that power must actually pass into the hands of the people at all levels. Government must continuously either recede into background or wither away, and its place must be taken up by the people themselves. Initiative must pass to the people. After independence, the people have become less independent, less self-restraint. We have to rely on the government for everything. Things have come to such a pass that we expect the government to do everything while we do nothing, not only in social and religious matter like untouchability, but even in our domestic affairs. A law may solve our problem but it will not make us stronger. What people really need is to become aware of their own inner strength, and that they can only do it they solve some of their problems for themselves.

Today in the name of the 'welfare state' we are concentrating all power at the centre. Even if the people do get a certain amount of benefit out of it, Vinoba would still call it not 'well-fare' but 'ill-fare' because it keeps power in the hands of a few. The idea of non-violence will spread only when power is shared among the villagers.

Decentralisation is not to be confined merely to industries. The process of decentralisation applies equally fruitfully to the authority of the state. Even thinkers who are avowedly intent on building up a non-violent social order at times lose sight of this fact. They support the demand for industrial decentralisation, but at the same time they often plead for a strong central authority for the preservation of the former. Vinoba submits that real freedom and peace can come only when people have established *Swaraj* or self-rule in small areas. Government will then be like a thread that keeps such self-sufficient and autonomous taluka units together. This is the only way of establishing peace in the world.

To quote Vinoba, "We want every village to have *swaraj*—to manage its own affairs. We want to see all powers vested in the village, so that the job of the State Government will not be to give orders to the village, but instead to keep the villages in touch with one another. In the same way the Government in Delhi would have no authority over the states, but would maintain contact between them. The higher the level of government, the more extensive would be the liaison work become, and the more limited would be its direct authority. The direct authority, the material power, will be exercised by the villages. The centre will be manned by persons of character and integrity who will thus exercise a moral authority. God practises this decentralisation. He has given all His creatures a share of intelligence—in the scorpion and the snake, to the tiger and the man. It is true that the shares are unequal, but each one has some and God has decreed that each one should direct its life by its own intelligence. As a result the world has got on so well that God has been able to take a holiday, and men have even begun to doubt His existence".[25]

We have fought against casteism and the practice of untouchability. Our fight against these evils is still going on. But a new division and casteism is becoming respectable. There are so many political parties. They grow like mushrooms and continue to sow seeds of division. Their function is to emphasise differences. A division of society among political warring groups in considered necessary for the growth of democracy. This artificial division in watertight separate parties has the sanction of political science. We have borrowed the apparatus, forms and institutions of democratic practice from the West. We have never cared to find out if they suited our ethos. The time has come when we have to re-examine and reassess the actual utility or value of some of the forms which we have adopted and are practising as a democratic ritual.

Where party politics are in vogue, one party holds all the power and another has none. The second is always contending with the first to get the power for itself. The party in power boasts to the people about its own great qualities and achievements; the opposition points out its shortcomings and mistakes. Every party speaks ill of the other parties; this absorption in fault-finding is the result of their worship of power. They all dance attendance on power, and worship at its altar, and there is a continual tug-of-war between them. Each party claims that if you return it to power, it will lead you to heaven, but that if you return the other fellows to power, they will lead you into hell. No one tells you the real truth—that your destiny, heaven or hell, is in your hands, and that no one but yourself can take you there. As long as this sort of thing goes on, there will be no contentment, no peace and no freedom in the world. People are fed up with parties which imply wasting of strength. One party weakens another party, and then this weakens the first one too. They both together weaken the country.

Political parties, whether in our country or outside, which subscribe to narrow ideals and loyalties, are out-of-date in this Age of Science. They are the remnants of an age which is fast disappearing. We have to understand that party politics is so narrow and useless a thing that it makes no sense today. The ill-will and jealousies that were confined in old times to a feudal chiefs or kings, have now been made countrywide by party politics. A party can come into existence only when there is an absence of right thinking.

It is the duty of *Sarvodaya* workers to stand between the rulers and the ruled, to point out mistakes on both sides, to foster mutual trust and understanding, and to increase the people's strength. They should identify themselves neither with the government nor with the people. They should be independent of both, and render true service to both, by pointing out the virtues and faults of both sides; they should be friends of all but be members of no party.

The majority method (of taking decisions) has come from the West and the Westerners consider it to be a progressive political idea. To us it appears to be a totally crude one. Perceiving truth has nothing to do with numerical majority. Formerly decisions were enforced on the point of sword; now-a-days they are enforced by a majority instead. We claim that we have give up the use of sword because it is an unintelligent way of doing things. But majority rule is not an intelligent way either. Matters cannot be rightly settled by counting heads; the only result is discontent and strife, and everyone is geared to the effort to overthrow one's opponent. At one time the minority ruled over the majority. It did not result in any good. As a reaction to it, emerged the rule of the majority over the minority. It is no pure love, but love born as a reaction. It has led to tensions in the world and given rise to the new problem of majority and minority everywhere.

Things will go rightly only when we accept the idea of unanimity. The Indian idea of a village *Panchayat* holds a special place among the political ideas of the world. It included the principle of 'God speaks through the five' which was accepted throughout India. This means that five members of the *Panchayat* must reach a common mind, and then only the decision was made. But now we 'pass' a decision by a majority of four to one or three to two, as though God speaks in the three! Vinoba contends that such proposals are not really passed, so long as they fail to convince even one person. Only that proposal deserves to 'pass' which commends itself to all. We must revive this ancient Indian tradition, for a people's democracy can only be built on mutual trust and cooperation. Truth and cooperation are essential to the prospering of its affairs. Without them, neither in India nor in the world can non-violence ever be maintained.

The increase of communal differences is the first evil consequence of elections. A second is that in the present set-up it is not possible for a man to stand for election unless he has wealth or property. We hold elections, but we do not even know our candidates by sight. Hundreds of thousands of people cast their votes, but so far from knowing the character of the man they vote for, they do not even know his face. For the sake of elections we spend our money, we allow the poison of communalism to spread, and in the end we have no guarantee that those elected will be worthy of our trust. The election has its own ethics. Its three principles are self-praise, speaking ill of others, and telling lies.

At least the present system of direct elections should be changed into that of indirect elections. For it, the party differences must be eliminated from the villages. There should be a general body consisting of all over twenty-one and it should elect an executive by unanimity. Unanimity and non-party village organisation are essential conditions for it. The higher bodies should be elected by *Gram Sabhas*, the village assemblies. Thus the elections should be indirect.

Whenever there are elections, no candidate of any party should be elected blindly. It is not right to elect an undeserving person simply because he belongs to one's own party. Elections do have some significance in the history of the country. But Vinoba wants to say that we have attached too much importance to politics. He does not say this about India only. He says it about the whole world. There would be no peace in the world as long as it gives that much importance to politics as it has given so far.

Sarvodaya does not mean good government or majority rule, it means freedom from government, it means decentralisation of power. We want to do away with government by politicians and replace it by a government of the people, based on love, compassion and equality. Decisions should be taken, not by majority, but by unanimous consent; and they should be carried out by the united strength of the ordinary people of the village.

Gram Panchayat is India's unique contribution to social thinking. In remote past when Europe had hardly awakened to social consciousness, we in India had made considerable progress in political and social thinking. The *Panchayat* system was evolved for dealing justice to all and providing protection and education to all. All had to submit to the unanimously agreed decisions of these councils. It can be regarded as a decentralised social order.

Village affairs would be managed by common consent, and not on any party basis. There would be a General Assembly of all villagers above the age of twenty-one. They would choose an executive committee of five, or seven, or ten members, which would run the administration of the village. But its decision would have to be unanimous. We have to make every village a complete and a thorough State in miniature. Thus, in every village there would be all the various departments as they are now in a State, such as Health, Industries, Agriculture, Education, Justice, etc. As there is a Foreign Affairs Department with respect to the relations with other countries, there will be in every village a special department which would handle the affairs pertaining to other villages.

The role of the Centre in a *Gram Swaraj* polity are the following: (1) The Central Government will be a link to keep the village republic together. (2) It will manage the railway, postal and such other services. (3) It will look after big industries and mines. (4) It will be in charge of defence and external relations, of the country. (5) It will be an overall advisory body. Powers will remain with the constituent republics. The central authority will gradually assume the shape of an advisory council.

Vinoba, outlined the programme for *Gram Panchayats*. He said, "Every Panchayat should organise a study circle which will acquaint the people of the village with new ideas and important developments taking place in the national and international fields. The Centre will specially provide for the study of Gandhian and *Sarvodaya* literature. Selected writings from such literature should be read out and explained to the people. The *Panchayats* should undertake to bring about an increase in production as one of their primary responsibilities. As long as the produce does not increase and the vast unemployment found in the villages is not liquidated, villagers are not likely to feel the urge for offering their cooperations to any developmental authority. The *Panchayat* should consider it their duty to see that no person within their areas remains unemployed and goes hungry. Just as the boycott of foreign goods helped the attainment of *Swaraj*, so would the boycott of mill cloth help bring about *Gramraj*. Since land is the basic factor of all production, the land must be distributed to all. The ownership of land should belong to the village and there should be no one without land. The real power of the *Panchayat* lies in the people's support.

The *Panchayats* should therefore follow their will and act under their control. They should not care whether the Government recognises them or not. The people must always rely on their own strength and go forward. The *Panchayats* should carry out these five functions. Then only will it be possible to establish *Ramrajya* in our villages".[26]

Isolation and separation, in the world today, means annihilation and death. Co-existence has become a condition for survival. Non-violence and brotherhood are no mere altruistic and idealistic concepts. They have the sanction of stark realism. Because of the phenomenal growth of science, brotherhood and love have acquired a new relevance. Society cannot last without them. If hate and rivalry continue as before, human society will be destroyed by modern science. If brotherhood and love become the cementing force in society, modern science will create a new world of freedom, peace and plenty.

The objective of *Sarvodaya* is to demolish the walls standing between various countries. Just as we are today free to move within India from one State to another, are welcome to live anywhere, can go for sight-seeing, education or business, similarly a man should be free to come and go to any place in the world. This is what we have to do. According to the non-violent way of thinking, human society is one, and in it separate nations are conceived of merely for the sake of convenience. If a particular nation has the good sense to adopt non-violence, it will not regard itself as separate from and as opposed to the others. It will be as anxious to safeguard the legitimate interests of neighbouring nations as those of its own.

Merely an absence of war is not peace. What is needed for peace is a constructive approach. These days absence of war is regarded as peace. But peace really connotes absence of fear. There would be peace only when no part of the world is afraid of or exploited by any other part. By peace Vinoba means something dynamic, something which will develop the power of the individual and the dynamic strength of the people to a degree that will enable them to meet any situation. *Shanti* or peace, therefore, cannot be negative. It has to be something positive.

Peace as wrongly understood in India is not peace but lack of sensitivity. What peace is there in lying calmly on a cushion bed. Peace has value when there are problems and efforts are being made to solve them. If peace means maintenance of *status quo*, that peace is worthless. Peace is something mental or spiritual. If there be peace in our life, it will affect the whole world.

Some advocates of peace point out that many nations of the world require peace today for they cannot develop themselves without it. Hence they desire peace in the world. Their movement is known as the World Peace Movement. There are several European countries which desire peace in spite of the communists being very strong there. As long as mankind has no independent thirst for peace, there can be no peace in the world. Another endeavour is also going on for the establishment of peace in the world. It is of the Moral Rearmament for which some people are collectively working. They try to go to other countries and to do something noble so that there be greater mutual love and friendliness. Non-violent resistance to war is the final result of a non-violent attitude and not the first as many Western pacifists seem to think.

It is wrong to think that a country's strength lies in its military power. A nation will become really strong only if it is free from internal conflicts, if it becomes self-sufficient and the people within are united by bonds of love. If we make our country strong like this, whatever be the threats or dangers that may confront us, none of them will cast any shadow on us. On the other hand, our greatness will certainly have a good influence on outside world. This country will have to be defended not by arms but by fearlessness, ethical behaviour and unity.

Nuclear weapons should, of course, be abolished. But the conventional weapons appear to be less frightening. The nuclear arms tend to bring us nearer to non-violence because they impel man to think and ponder. But pistols and daggers put non-violence far away. These weapons appear to be small, but they are the parents of nuclear arms. Renunciation of arms can take place only when there will be a plan for decentralised production. It cannot happen earlier. *Sarvodaya* thought is worthless if the *Sarvodayees* feel that army is indispensable. It will be an act of wisdom as well as courage if India reduces her armament. This act will enhance her reputation and prestige in the world. It will make her powerful in the real sense.

We should create such conditions in the country that the police or the army becomes unnecessary for internal peace. If we can achieve this, the next step of the extension of non-violence to external defence, would become apparent. For peace and security within the country, we must cast off mutual differences and share our weal and woe together. Sharing decreases misery and increases joy.

Vinoba does not believe in dividing men as criminals and non-criminals. To him, no man is a criminal. Some men are branded as such and are put in jails. But some criminals are to be found outside—only they are not so in the eyes of law. It is held that the pleader, the judge and the police etc., work to eradicate crimes and robberies. But they are all of the same fraternity as thieves and robberies. They punish the innocent and feed the culprit.

People are afraid that crime will increase if a deterrent like capital punishment is abolished. Those who know something of the psychology of a criminal will understand that a deterrent like capital punishment hardly enters his mind when he is seized by some insane passion. Our civilisation and culture have looked upon public opinion as the final sanction of right social behaviour. It is not the penal code that keeps men and women on the right path. The existence of proper values and public opinion is an effective guide to good conduct. In an ideal *Sarvodaya* society law will not need a penal code. It will express itself as the conscience of the people.

To quote Vinoba, "There are always in society a few noble individuals who do not require public opinion to hold them within the limits of morality. Similarly there are also wayward and indiscriminate individuals who, unmindful of public opinion, go against the laws of morality. But the general public or the great majority of people observe what is ordained and avoid what is prohibited by public opinion. Such public opinion naturally constitutes the basis of law or restraint, and the vast majority of people always respect it. The few wayward individuals who remain outside the number should be put in the company of the few who are high souled, instead of being submitted to forcible restraint."[27]

It is obvious that if we are really anxious to eradicate crime, then we must find out its root cause which lies in the faulty organisation of society. We must purify and where necessary rebuild the social organisation. Simultaneously with the purification of the social organisation, there must also be purification of thought. Efforts should be made to introduce and establish in our social consciousness the idea that it is a sin to hoard wealth and avoid physical labour. Love, compassion, generosity and forgiveness have a higher place in life as moral attributes than hard-hearted punishment.

The basic problem of the world today is the establishment of peace. Perhaps in no other age has there been such a world-hunger for peace. Today there is an explosive situation in the country. There can be a sudden explosion for any reason whatsoever. The Shanti Sena is not a new proposal. We owe both the world and the idea behind it to

Gandhiji, who himself endeavoured to give it a practical shape. He was both its commander and its first soldier.

The Shanti Sena is an army which offers its services in perpetuity to all men without distinction. To be a Shanti Sainik means to be prepared to leave everything, home, public work, etc., and go wherever he may be called. This is one point in which he differs from other *Lok Sevaks;* has other pledges are the same. The work of the Shanti Sainik has therefore two aspects: his regular, day-to-day duties are of a 'Seva Sainik' while his occasional duties are those of the Shanti Sainik. It is not the duty of the Shanti Sainik to find solutions for all problems of society. His job is to help people in their physical troubles, and do his best to help them also in their mental worries. In addition, he will be taking every chance of helping them to understand the ideas of *Bhoodan*, *Gramdan*, etc., and bringing *Sarvodaya* literature to their notice.

Those who enlist in the Shanti Sena will consider it their duty to serve the whole community, to help all the needy, without regard for caste, religion, sect, party or any other distinction. The Shanti Sainik must treat everyone, high or low, in the same way; like water he must be humble, gentle, clean, pure and cool. The first requirement for a Shanti Sainik is that no one should be afraid of him. The various political parties also must have no fear of him; if they are afraid, he must show by his conduct that he has no partisan spirit, that he is out to serve without looking for any reward, and that he has no inclination to join any party but is working only for *Sarvodaya*, the welfare of all, and is ready to give his life, if need arise, in that cause.

A member of Shanti Sena, whether a man or woman, must have a living faith in non-violence. This is only possible if one has a living faith in God. This messenger of peace should have equal respect for all the prominent religions of the world. He should have the knowledge of the principles common to various religions. The Shanti Sainik accepts the principle of *aparigrah*a (non-possession), and does not accumulate unnecessary possessions. But this does not mean that he must give up all he has.

The main principal of Shanti Sena is that they should be free from partisanship, free from hatred, free from fear. They will trust one another, will fear none, and will frighten none. They will consider no man their enemy; their hearts will be filled with love. This is the pledge of the Shanti Sainik. It is necessary that Shanti Sainiks are trained for their work. Some portions of the primary training of the army is also essential.

It is about discipline, drill, chorus singing etc. A volunteer should know how to remove the wounded. He should have such articles with him as are needed for First Aid. He should know how to extinguish fire, how to enter safely a place on fire, how to climb up with or without a load and to descend safely. For increase of knowledge, refresher courses should also be arranged. They should teach the worker how he can serve the best. The member should have a special dress so that they may be identified without any difficulty.

If women will take up the work of Shanti Sena, the face of the world will change, and we shall be able to achieve freedom from the problems which we are facing today in the country and abroad. In this age of science, when men's brains have become paralysed, if our women come forward with their divine qualities of restraint and modesty, and use their mother-power, they can establish the rule of compassion. In the path of violence, men will always lead. But in the path of non-violence, women can go ahead of them. So it is essential that women should lead, and that too in their own way.

Legislation and coercion will not create a happy and free man. If we want a radical change, we have to bring about a change in the heart and mind of man. We have to appeal to every individual and open his eyes to the new truth. If we leave everything to the government, we cripple ourselves. The government enacts laws, but the laws cannot discriminate. There is a place for legislation in non-violence, but it will not serve its purpose unless there is a congenial climate for it.

REFERENCES

1. *Gandhi Marg*, November-December 1983, pp. 436-438.
2. Suresh Ram, *Vinoba and His Mission*, p. 292.
3. T.N. Atreya, *Dharma Samanvaya*, p. 140.
4. *Ibid.*, p. 120.
5. *Ibid.*, p. 48-49.
6. Vinoba Bhave, *The Principles and Philosophy of the Bhoodan Yagna*, p. 41.
7. *Bhoodan*, 23-5-1956, p. 7.
8. *Vinoba Chintan*, No. 7, p. 9.
9. *Ramanam Ek Chintan*, pp. 38-39.
10. *The Harijan*, 9-4-1955, p. 41.
11. *Prarthana Pravachan*, 17-2-1957.
12. *The Harijan*, 16-10-1949, p. 278.
13. *Sarvodaya*, August 1950, p. 141.
14. *The Steadfast Wisdom*, p. 80.
15. *Kranti Ki Rah Par*, p. 73.
16. *Vinoba Pravachan*, 14-5-1959.

17. *Gandhi Marg*. November-December 1983. p. 467.
18. *Ibid.*
19. *Samya-Sutra*, p. 49.
20. *Bhoodan Yajna*. 8-10-1965.
21. *Maitri*. October 1982, p. 883.
22. *Third Power*, p. 21-22.
23. *The Harijan*. 25-12-1949, p. 374.
24. *Vinoba Pravachan*, 10-12-1959.
25. *Democratic Values*, pp. 105-108.
26. *The Harijan*, 11-9-1954, p. 228.
27. *Swaraj Shastra*, p. 35.

3

ON SARVODAYA

Gandhiji's idea of trusteeship was translated into action by his disciple Vinoba. He gave life to the concept by introducing the *Bhoodan* and *Gramdan* movement. Gandhiji has considered Vinoba as his spiritual heir. The task of translating the *Sarvodaya* philosophy into a plan of action was taken by Vinoba in the shape of *Bhoodan* movement, which took the shape of *Gramdan* and *Sampatidan*.

The *Bhoodan* movement was started by Vinoba on 15 April, 1951 in the Telangana region of Andhra Pradesh. The reason for starting this movement was a violent struggle between the landlords and the landless for land. Under the guidance of Vinoba, Akhil Bharathiya Sarva Seva Sangh took up the challenge to translate into reality the objectives of the *Sarvodaya* philosophy. The basic objective of *Bhoodan* has been to inspire the people to develop a selfless attitude and feelings for the good of the masses. Gandhiji said, "What *Bhoodan* says about land is true of all our possessions, including even knowledge and skill. All wealth is a social product and no earning is possible without social cooperation. Whatever we possess, therefore, belongs to the society. We are no more than trustees of what we have, implicitly charged by the society to take good care of our own trust and use it for the benefit not of ourselves but of all our fellow men".[1]

The concept of *Bhoodan* is based on the principle of a partyless democracy. Vinoba remarked, "In a sense *Bhoodan* is itself an intensely and deeply political movement. A movement that aims so utterly to revolutionise man and society cannot be but political. But it is politics of the kind I have described above—not the politics of parties, elections, parliaments and governments; but politics of the people—not *Rajniti* but *Lokniti*".[2]

Bhoodan does not aim merely at getting land from the people and distributing it among the landless. It tries to abolish the gap between the haves and have-nots through non-violent means of *Satya* and *Ahimsa*. Love and cooperation should be the basic principles governing the individual and social behaviour. Social justice and equality should be the main objective. To quote Jayaprakash Narayan, "First of all, we must realise that *Bhoodan* is not a programme of merely collecting and distributing land. It is rather the first step towards total revolution—social, political and economic. It stands for a society which would strive for the good of all, and in which everybody would be happy. In such a society there should be no distinction of high and low. Justice and equality would form its distinguishing features and exploitation in any form would be completely eliminated. Power and authority would vest with the people in the true sense, they would regulate and administer their own affairs. Central authority would be sought to be extinguished, and if is continued to exist, the sphere and extent of its operations would be minimised. The village will have all the authority and jurisdiction required."[3]

The *Bhoodan* believes in universal brotherhood, which starts from the lowest level. Starting from the individual it extends to the village, the nation and, ultimately the whole world. Jayaprakash Narayan said, "*Bhoodan* is thus a great mass movement of conversion and the creation of a new climate of thought and value of life. It brings about a living and immediate revolution in the minds of men and their mutual relationships. It attacks and corrects here and now the system of exploitation and inequality. It teaches men to share what they have with their fellowmen."[4]

Dan does not imply charity because the feeling of charity is against the spirit of equality and brotherhood. Jayaprakash Narayan said, "Bhoodan is not a charity movement, that behind it is Mahatma Gandhi's theory of trusteeship, in other words, the simple yet potent truth that man is not the master of what he possesses but only a trustee of what in reality belongs to the society".[5]

In 1951, the Third Anniversary Sarvodaya Conference of constructive workers was held in Hyderabad. Vinoba preferred to cover the three hundred miles from Wardha to Hyderabad on foot. Reaching Hyderabad for the conference, Vinoba was fully prepared for confronting the challenges ahead. On the last day of the conference, i.e. 11 April, 1951, he expressed the desire to tour the communist-infested areas of Telangana district chiefly for the purpose of propagating the message of peace and harmony. He wanted to study the facts at first hand, before returning to Wardha. "What would happen during this sojourn or thereafter was known only to God," remarked Vinoba. Leaving Shivrampalli he reached Hyderabad and took the opportunity of meeting some communists in jail and he had a very frank and cordial talk with them. He visited the village of Pochampalli comprising of 90 families. He rested for a while in the village school building, got up suddenly and walked and started his round with the Harijan colony and entered several cottages to see their plight with his own eyes. The Harijans surrounded him and entreated: "We are very poor, we are also unemployed and therefore unhappy. Please help us".

"In what way can I help you?" enquired Vinoba. "We want only work and nothing else. Please give us some land, so that we may work hard on it to eke out our livelihood." Vinoba, not knowing what to do, asked them, "How much land do you really require?"

After conferring among themselves for a while one of them said: "Only 80 acres will do. We are 40 families, and two acres for each family will be quite adequate for our purpose". In this way the landless people in that village approached him and asked for his help in getting land for cultivation for their sustenance. Vinoba began to think seriously about this matter, but no solution was in sight. He, therefore, quietly said, "I will find out from the Government whether it is possible to allot any land for you. This is a difficult question. Even so, I will try to explore the possibilities". And then, it suddenly struck him that someone in the village audience in the evening prayer meeting may like to donate some land for these poor *Harijans*. He lifted his eyes at the gathering, and remarked rather casually, "Brothers, is there anybody amongst you who can help these Harijan friends?" Surprisingly, one Mr. Ramachandra Reddy came forward to donate 100 acres of land. Ramachandra Reddy stood, up, looked at Vinoba with folded hands and said, "Please do accept my donation of 100 acres". Neither Vinoba nor the members of his party could believe these words. But Ramachandra Reddy, continued standing with his hands folded and awaiting Vinoba's concurrence. Vinoba was overwhelmed with emotion. It was, really a miracle. The *Harijans* asked for only 80 acres, and the donor spontaneously offered 100 acres. After wiping the tears with his upper cloth, Vinoba said, "I have come here with empty hands and will proceed to the next village tomorrow morning again with empty hands. Both the donor and the donee are present here in our midst. Let them exchange the land in our presence. The donor should also help the Harijan friends with some money and implements for cultivating the land in cooperative way". Ramachandra Reddy gently bowed before

Vinoba and accepted the responsibility. The Harijans also touched his feet with joy and satisfaction. Vinoba had no words to thank the donor. Apart from evoking an immediate response for solving problems presented to him, it also gave birth to a highly revolutionary strategy based on peaceful co-existence, i.e. *Bhoodan* movement.

The following excerpts from Vinoba highlight his imagination and future plan for solving the land problem in India. "That night when I went to bed I could not sleep. I was thinking over the event. What has happened to me today? I am a mathematician, I began to work but how much land would be needed for all the landless people in India. I came to the conclusion that fifty crore, fifty million acres, will be required for distribution, that is one-sixth of all cultivable land in India. I could not believe that people would offer that amount of land. The idea had come to me and attacked me, and my mind tried to resist because I was not ready to accept. And so I hesitated. But a voice from within myself told me that if I doubt, I do not put my faith in the power of love and God. Then I must abandon my belief in non-violence and follow the violent way of the communists. You can't sit quiet any longer. You must either go this way or that way. God puts the hunger into the child's belly and he also puts the milk into the mother's breast; so if you go begging in the name of God, you will get a response".

> "But I had only a hundred acres of land in my hand, and this was a question of asking for fifty million acres. I did not consult any of my friends or any institution because they would have said that I may expect to get thousands of acres, but I could not expect to get millions—so I decided to go ahead, by myself, to start begging for land and to see how people respond".
>
> "The next day in the morning I started for the next village. The village people had prepared breakfast for me. I told them that I won't breakfast, I won't break my fast while my countrymen are hungry; give me a few acres of land for my breakfast. And God's will was there and they gave me twenty-five acres".

This was the birth of the great *Bhoodan* movement. The sudden miracle at Pochampalli village thrilled his whole being and Vinoba clearly recognised the hand of God in this unforeseen event. Addressing the village gathering after prayers, he remarked, "Man does not act merely on the strength of his own thinking. There is always a Divine had behind such noble actions. I am a man of faith, and work for me. I will walk from village to village to seek land donations for the poor". He turned on foot asking for land donations.

With other gifts in hand, Vinoba used his evening prayer meeting to speak of land gift as *Bhoodan* and to expand on the significance of *dan*. Referring to an afternoon conversation with a villager, he said, "A brother began to say that in the village some people are very poor and some people are rich. But it is like this in every village. Some people are rich and a lot are poor. Between them, the rich and the poor, there are quarrels. I have a way to erase these. What is this way? It is this: Keep giving what you have as *dan*. God has given us these two hands, and he has given them in order that we can give *dan* to others. God Shri Krishna has pointed out this way in the *Gita*. He said that it is required for every person that he should give some of what he has to others as *dans*. If we give *dan* it is reproduced tenfold and the world is happy. And if we do not give *dan* and keep everything for ourselves, the whole country becomes unhappy".[6] He saw *bhoodan* as a general solution to the problem of extreme economic inequality.

When Vinoba elaborated on the ideal village, he made it clear that he had not abandoned his view that the maintenance of traditional virtues came before the demand for equality. He said, "All you people, please begin to serve one another. The task of workers is to give the owner a full day's work. The owner's obligation is to feed the workers first, and afterwards to eat himself. This was the way in this country in the old days. The owner first fed his workers, his cows, his bullocks, in short everybody, and then ate. This is the sign of a big man. Like a mother and a father he cares for everybody. But today the big man is the one who exploits others. It is as if he eats his own children. This is the mark of a demon. In big people there should be generosity, in small people there should be humility. If there is generosity, love and humility, God's blessings will certainly come to this village".[7]

On 29 April, 1951, Vinoba also went beyond land to say that wealth and everything belonged to everyone. He said, "Nowadays everybody is giving land, and you should also give your share. If you have land, you should give some land. If you have wealth, you should give some wealth. Wealth is not only money. Those who have books should give books; those who have time should give *samay-dan*; those who have strength should give *shram-dan*; those who have knowledge should give *buddhi-dan*. But it should be the case that everyone has given".[8] On 12 May, 1951, he added to the list by asking a group of urban *Zamindars* and intellectuals to give their lives for the sake of villagers.

Vinoba focused on *bhoodan* in such a way that it became as much a symbol for personal transformation as a solution to the land problem. On 20 May, 1951, he said, "Before whenever there were disturbances in the country, our wise men used to start a *yajna*. When I entered this region it occurred to me that I also should start a *yajna*. Here there are quarrels, violence, murder. . . . But what sort of *yajna*, I thought. At first it did not occur to me. Should an animal sacrifice be started? But what benefit can man derive from an animal sacrifice? If there is to be benefit, then it is from destroying the animals of desire, anger, greed and ignorance. These are also animals, the ones which rule our minds. So we should sacrifice these animals—such a *yajna* is possible. I these times, I wondered, which animal most influences our heart. I realised the most developed animal, the one that gives us the most difficulty, is material greed. Today not many lions live in the jungle, and therefore, they do not give us much trouble. But this animal called greed is giving lots of trouble, giving trouble everywhere. By sacrificing this animal, peace is possible. Then I began to place the demand for *bhumidan* before you. Wherever I have gone people have understood that this animal called greed should be sacrificed. People have not completely renounced greed, nevertheless they have given a little *bhumidan*. In this *bhumidan-yajna* everyone should take a small part. Whenever some public *yajna* is started, everyone has to take part. When someone starts any great public *yajna*, he should get a cup of milk from each home. If some *raja* or rich man gives most of the milk, it will not succeed. In this *bhumidan-yajna* each person should take part. This is because the goal is the inner purification of everyone."[9]

Vinoba began asking people to consider him or the poor or society as an additional member of their family and to share accordingly. He said, "Everyone should vow that he will immediately give to a man who has nothing and who comes to ask for something. You should understand that this man who demands things is a rightful claimant. If a new child is born to a poor house, what will the poor people do? First there were three in the house and now there are four, and so they will divide among the four and eat. Therefore, we people should understand that there are five children in our house and this sixth child is society. Whether, he be poor or rich, a person you should understand that however many persons there are in his home, there is one more and he should set aside this extra person's share. If in any house there is an estate of 6,00,000 and five persons, then this estate should be divided into six parts and it should be understood that this sixth part is society's. If in any house there is an estate of five rupees, then this also is to be divided like this."[10]

Gradually the message of the peaceful and non-violent revolution spread into other parts of the country and it gained momentum in course of time in various states. *Padayatras* were organised for propagating the message and collecting the lands to be distributed to the landless. Vinoba was fully convinced that if this scheme is implemented on a nation-wide scale, there would be no land problem as there would be enough land for distribution among the landless poor.

In every village, land donations poured in, and Vinoba was convinced that God wanted him to continue this movement tirelessly with faith and resolution. The historic Telangana tour lasted for 51 days and Vinoba passed through some 200 villages and received 12,200 acres of land for distribution among the landless. Not a single village refused to give the gifts, the average being 240 acres a day. Even after Vinoba left Telangana, the local workers were able to collect a further, 1,00,000 acres as a result of the tempo created by the *Bhoodan* mission. Returning from Telangana, Vinoba reached Paramdham Ashram on 26 June, 1951, and he received an invitation from the Prime Minister, to advise the Planning Commission at Delhi. He decided to start for Delhi on foot. He also wanted to test the *Bhoodan* idea in areas, which were not haunted by Communists. During the first week of this *Padayatra*, he covered about 110 miles and obtained 2000 acres of land, an average of little less than 300 acres per day.

The State governments passed Bhoodan Yajna Acts. The State Bhoodan Boards were formed to look after the *bhoodan* and redistribution. The allottees who receive the *Bhoodan* lands should cultivate them within three years, otherwise, the Bhoodan Boards would take away those lands. Though the allottees would have the full rights of enjoyment and rights of inheritance, they cannot sell, mortgage or lease them out.

Even when statutory efforts were being made, Vinoba was adamant that he would accept only what is given with love. He did not consider the scheme as a success, if lands were given unwillingly by big land-owners. In the second phase, therefore, he approached the middle class land-owners and explained the purpose of *Bhoodan* and prospects it can bring in. He appealed to them with examples quoted from the epics such as Sudama's small gifts of rice to Lord Krishna. He was certain that all have the capacity to give a small portion which will produce the desired effect in helping the landless. He was more keen to bring in change among the landlords than on the stress laid on the number of acres they donate. He was happy that "everyone's heart is changing" and observes that "if all hearts can change in this manner, legislation will not be necessary. The whole problem can be solved with love".

Vinoba's main task was to propagate the idea that all wealth including the lands belong to everyone. He expected the constructive workers to act as catalysts in society so as to bring in a meaningful social revolution. *Bhoodan* is an all-embracing revolution that seeks to bring about an overall transformation of human values and thus establishes a new order wherein the individual interest will exist only as a part of the wider social interest. In 1958, Vinoba had kept the target of collecting 50 million acres of land. He could reach to a level of 4.2 million acres of land and this could achieve a partial success of 8.4 percentage. However, it should not be analysed from a quantitative view, but the qualitative change that was brought is more meaningful and long lasting. Compared to the governmental efforts, through legislation which yielded only 2.2 million acres of land, Vinoba's efforts proved to be a better success.

The ideological basis of the movement is that whatever people have is like trust and should be held and used as such, whatever it is land or any other kind of property, or whether it is knowledge, skill or experience. It is not meant for their personal enjoyment alone; everyone has a share in it. It is by propagating the philosophy of Love and Truth, and by persuading people to regard themselves and live as one family that Vinoba has aimed at bringing about a non-violent agrarian revolution, The movement thus arose by the surrender of part of a person's land but in course of time partial sharing developed into total sharing. But, this concept of sharing of Vinoba has made universal and many important extensions of the idea have taken place in all other spheres of life of man and society. The *Bhoodan* movement may be looked at as a concrete manifestation of the application of the universal principle of Love, Truth and Non-violence to India's practical problems. The *Bhoodan* movement aims to prepare the ground work for an agrarian economy, wherein land ceases to be a marketable commodity and where the individual workers are to attain the good of the entire community. This is just one step towards the realisation of real democracy by setting right the inverted structure of economic centralisation through practices based on the principles of love and non-violence. Decentralisation of political as well as economic power is the essence of the movement.[11]

The economic structure of our society resembles an inverted pyramid. The millions of the have-nots and the landless at the base are at present unable to form into any solid foundation for a permanent and stable economic structure. It is of importance that the base of the structure must be broadened by uniting the poor masses and the top heavy layers suitably built in conformity with the basic structure. At the village level, the pyramid like structure begins with the landless masses at the base with rich peasants and big land-owners above them in that ascending order. The benefits are sucked out at the level of the big land-owners and rich peasants, a little reaches down to the poor and nothing to the landless. Obviously such a structure, whether on the level of the economy as a whole or on the village level, cannot be stable; nor can it be conducive to higher production and to the establishment of the balanced community life. It is necessary, that the broad upper levels of the structure are saved-off and large portions of the vast upper levels of the structure are brought down to earth, narrow at the top and broad at the bottom. This is just like concentric circle of wave in the water or a pond each circle broadening without being a burden to each other. This involves the process of economic decentralisation.

Vinoba contended that the problems of landless should be solved first, as it would provide a solid foundation to the village economic structure. For this, it is necessary that ownership of land, property or resources must be recognised as nature's or God's, that one who consumes must do some productive physical labour. The *Bhoodan*, therefore, demands from the rich peasants one sixth of their land and the poor peasants are also asked to donate whatever they can as a token of their acceptance of the *bhoodan*. And as it is a '*dan*', it contends for the just equitable distribution of land among one and all; it requires the donor to do his duty towards himself and his neighbours and it insists that all should work on land and none should keep it, who does not work. Thus economic decentralisation is one of the ends of the movement. The ultimate objective is the setting up of decentralised self-sufficient units, where the villages will decide their affairs themselves. But, first things, first, and hence the first priority to the problem of land.

It is the economy of service making for peace, permanence and non-violence that the *bhoodan* aims at. In this economy, the sense of duty, not only to those of the group but to all creatures, pervades the whole. The motivation here is the good of others even if it may be seemingly detrimental to self-interest. The emphasis in this economy is more on duties than on rights. It is based on love and spirit of service and self-sacrifice, leading the community to happiness and peace through the medium of non-violence. Gandhiji tried to evolve a socio-economic order in which the principle of love, self-sacrifice and renunciation were to be used as norms both of daily living and human behaviour. He made love and non-violence instruments of an all-embracing social revolution.

it has fallen to the lot of Vinoba to give a practical shape to Gandhiji's principles. Not that Gandhiji had not evolved that concept of an economy based on his enunciated principles but his political preoccupations somehow precluded the translation of those principles into practice. Vinoba as the spiritual successor of Gandhiji picked up the thread, where the master had left and went ahead with experimenting with the concrete manifestations of the universal principles of love and sacrifice. The application of these principles in the socio-economic sphere brought home to Vinoba the curious fact that it was the right of ownership engendered by the insatiable instinct of acquisitiveness that was the root of all economic, political and social ill. That is why *bhoodan* movement aims not merely at the transfer and redistribution of land from the landed to the landless, but its ultimate objective is the complete abolition of the deep-rooted concept of ownership, whether of land, capital or skill. The quest of Vinoba's *bhoodan* movement, therefore, is for the establishment of new values in society. The land-gift mission is just an external symbol of the aimed transformation of the inner-most values of human behaviour. The ultimate end is the evolution of an economy based on the principles of love, renunciation and sacrifice wherein the good of the individual shall consists in the welfare of all. The structure of such a communitarian economy shall have an extended family pattern, its character will be all-inclusive, its behaviour well grounded in voluntary surrender and mutual sharing and its end the greatest good of one and all.

The present age demands equality; equality as between friends and comrades. Vinoba was out to build the *Sarvodaya* order or what he calls *Sama-yoga*. He had a great talent for coining words and investing old words with new meanings. Thus 'd*an*' in his vocabulary did not mean gifts but, "sharing together". *Dan* has so far meant giving of something by an act of piety or charity. However, he used it to mean distribution based on justice and equality, as one finds among the different members in a joint family. He did not demand *dan* by force. He believed in *ahimsa* and never compelled the person to give, if he was not willing to do so. "Give by love, give by capacity, by reason". He did not use the word *dan* for land-gift mission alone. He created some other types of *dans* also. In short, five types of *dans*: (1) *Bhoodan*—to change the basic concept of ownership and to generate self-sufficient village economy; (2) *Sampatidan*—towards equal distribution of wealth, discording the accumulation of wealth and abolishing unproductive labour and its trade; (3) *Sharamdan*—to establish the dignity of labour, love, purity and interest in work and to make even the landless to participate in social reconstruction and contribute their shares in it; (4) *Premdan*—a purely human and moral act, requiring one to love they neighbour as thyself; (5) *Buddhidan*—those who are intellectually equipped but are poor and frail can devote some of their time to help with their knowledge and wisdom. Persons like teachers, doctors and lawyers, specialists can offer their free service for the good of the society.

Vasant Nargolkar, while admitting the achievements of the *Bhoodan* movement says that the movement failed to fulfil the expectations it has originally aroused. It failed to solve the land problems, to have any impact on the social, economic and political situation in India, to influence the thinking of the intelligentsia. He attributed this failure to the rejection of *satyagraha*, as a means of bringing about a non-violent revolution. There was no enthusiastic participation of the people and no involvement of the people in *Gramdan* villages in the difficult task of promoting *Sarvodaya* ideals. Nargolkar is not opposed to Vinoba's technique, but he would like to supplement it by direct non-violent action. Since *Sarvodaya* rejected parliamentary programme, it is all the more necessary to retain the effective weapon of people's active participation and cooperation. When all is said and done, a feeling persists that it would have been better, if *satyagraha* in the form of non-violent resistance had found a greater scope in the *Sarvodaya* a movement. It is indeed ironical that none in the *Sarvodaya* movement or outside has yet been able to discover the form of non-violent resistance suitable for the present day realities of India. However, the concept of gentle and gentler *satyagraha* is a great contribution of Vinoba and it would be in interests of both India and other countries, if extensive research work and experiments are undertaken in the above directions—especially in agrarian problems.[12]

Land is the gift of God and according to an old adage "all land belongs to Gopal". So, in the divine dispensation land rightly belongs to him who works on it. In ancient times land belonged to the village community, and the village panchayat distributed the same to the village people every 20 or 25 years, in accordance with the number of members in a family. This was dictated by the principle that nobody should have more land than he required. This applies equally to other forms of wealth as well. For nobody produces wealth singly by his own effort.

We have an insight into the political theory of the *Bhoodan* movement. It does not aim at capturing the state in order to use it for its ends. It insists that if our ultimate aim is to do without the state, we must here and now create those conditions in which the people will rely more and more on themselves and less and less on the state. A movement that aims so utterly to revolutionise man and society cannot be but political. But, it is not politics of parties, elections, parliaments and governments, but policies of the people not *raj-niti* but *lok-niti,* as Vinoba said. It is making a valuable political experiment. It aims ultimately to create a non-party democracy. It does not rely on the action of the people. Governments follow the people and put the seal of approval on what they have already done. As Gandhiji said, legislation comes after conversion. That is why Vinoba is not shouting for legislation. He knows that after people have acted, legislation is bound to follow, no matter which party is in power.

A real and lasting change in the social order can be brought about only by a real change of heart and we should take a lesson in that respect from the French and Russian revolutions. Misery in the world is not due to shortage of provisions and amenities, which science can multiply to any extent but due to the narrowness and possessiveness of man. There is misery not because there is no production but man is self-centred and does not think of others. This sort of life results in preparation of war. The problems seemingly political are in fact moral. The possessive instinct has to be weeded out by all. Rich and poor alike are victims of the craving for acquiring wealth, both adore the same values. That is why Vinoba insisted on receiving *Bhoodan* even from small land-holder and *sampatidan* from everybody, rich and poor.

Bhoodan is not a sectional, rural, national movement, though it may have local application. It is universally applicable to the entire human race. It aims at the good of all which includes your good also. If everyone's good is achieved, your good is also automatically achieved.

Every man is born with certain potentialities and tendencies, of good and bad qualities. Our good consists in your being guaranteed fullest possible scope for the development of all virtues in us. If we are given the opportunity everyone can achieve his good. The message of *bhoodan* is that you should share whatever you have, land, property, intellect, etc., with your neighbours. Ultimately, every village will become an enlarged family. The every nation, and the whole world would become one family.

The *Bhoodan* movement has been weak on the publicity front. There are not many journals and books on the subject. Adequate information is not available about the development work done by *bhoodan* lands. Lack of facts and figures in detail regarding development work done in this sphere makes it difficult to present an overall assessment. *Bhoodan* is a mass movement and that people themselves should organise it, the *Samitis* were dissolved. So, the *Bhoodan* movement has not been able to catch the imagination of the masses as it was expected of it. The slow moving legislative machinery should be geared up. The farmers who had donated the land were forced to pay the revenue for land given away by them because of the time consuming processes involved in making the transfer legal. This made their donors taking back their land from tenants earlier given by them in the *bhoodan*. The small size of holding distributed to the landless with improper and insufficient facilities for even an ordinary utilisation forced them to abandon the land so received in the *Bhoodan* movement. Another factor which can contribute to the success of the movement is the help from the government. The government can help the movement by providing persons capable of carrying out development activities. It can provide the needed trained technical personnel to carry out the projects, government aid is desirable for the successful implementation of the *bhoodan* plans. But then the government should have no power to interfere with the working of the movement.

Some of the Criticism about *Bhoodan* movement are as follows:

1. Absence of clarity regarding the objectives of the movement.
2. Lopsided approach to the agrarian problem. It aims to help and provide land only to the landless villagers.
3. The movement provides insufficient land to the landless.
4. It leads to the division and fragmentation of already small and scattered fields.
5. It creates uneconomic holdings. As poor person join the movement by donating a small piece of land from their already

tiny plots, the holdings are reduced to uneconomic units.

6. Most of the land donated is of inferior quality and some of it is extremely poor.
7. It will hardly be successful in rehabilitating all the landless agricultural labourers.
8. The slogan "land to the landless" seems to emphasise the indispensable character of land for those who do not have it.
9. It stands in the way of mechanised farming. The small five acres holdings that the *bhoodan* aims at providing to the landless of the country are unsuitable for mechanised farming.
10. Its machinery is not efficient and the distribution process is very slow.
11. The target for land-gift was set at fifty million acres which was to be achieved by the end of 1957. It was too high an ambition for a voluntary movement depending entirely on moral persuasion. Up to the end of 1957, only one-tenth of the target fixed has been achieved,
12. It was claimed by the protagonists of *bhoodan* that they were not enamoured of collectivisation and they intended rather to give land to the millions of landless labourers in the countryside on an individual or family basis to begin with.

Bhoodan was followed by *gramdan. Gramdan*, literally means "village gift" whereas *bhoodan* means "land gift". The *bhoodan* movement gave birth to *gramdan*. The *gramdan* was first put into operation in September 1952, in a village named Mangroth in Uttar Pradesh. Under the *gramdan*, the resources of the village are to be exploited equally by each and every member of the village community. The entire village community works for its prosperity and welfare. Jayaprakash Narayan said, "I will believe that as people join *gramdan* and gather some strength, corruption will come to an end. I do not say that no corruption ever took place in the *gramdan* village or the government officials, overseers, etc. . . . But if you compare them with other villages, there is a world of difference. This is why there is some hitch over *gramdan* from their side".[13] For social and economic progress, the *gramdan* movement is at the top of all other programmes. Jayaprakash Narayan said, "The changes that can be brought about even in the initial stages by *gramdan* are of such a vital character as cannot be obtained by any amount of official work, or programmes of political parties, or activities of Panchayat Raj or Community

Development or Five Year Plans. . . . All these programmes will never be able to match in quality or quantity, the attainments of *gramdan*."[14]

Vinoba entered the village Mangroth and this proved to be a red letter day in the annals of *Bhoodan* movement. The residents of the village presented him with 101 acres of land. He accepted the gift and repeated—"all land belongs to God". With this message in their hearts, they returned home to consider his appeal. Diwan Shatrughan Singh was a devoted constructive worker. In the post-prayer meeting at Mangroth, he announced his decision to donate whole of his land to *bhoodan*. The villagers also agreed to join the movement. Mangroth, thus earned the distinction of being the first *gramdan* village. The total number of families in that village was 107. After the declaration of *gramdan*, the land belonged to the village and all the families decided to work with their hands and jointly enjoyed the fruits of cultivation. The planning of the crops was to be decided by the Village Panchayat in order to achieve self-sufficiency in foodgrains and vegetables.

According to G. Ramachandran, "*Gramdan* means a large fund of unity of mind in the village, a readiness to face practical changes in the social and economic structure of the village, the courage to walk on a new road and readiness on the part of the individual to make a sacrifice in favour of the community and, therefore, something precise, unambiguous and challenging in the confused situation affecting the rural areas today. . . . *Gramdan* is a mental and economic revolution representing the reassertion of modern world. *Gramdan* is a complete break-away from the tradition of private ownership of land which has been the rock upon which the life of the village in India has rested during uncounted centuries. And yet, the entire spirit underlying *gramdan* is in harmony with the spirit of the culture of India which has always put renunciation for above power".

According to Shriman Narayan, "It is revolutionising the basic values of life and the method for achieving the objective is through non-violence, democracy and conversion of hearts in place of classwar, hatred and violence. Moreover, the *Bhoodan* and the *Gramdan* movements are able to touch the most backward and poorest sections of the population. It is being realised on all hands that over development schemes have not been able so far to ameliorate the economic condition of the lowest sections of our people. . . . The cooperating way in *Gram Raj* is able to touch the felt needs of the poorest sections in an effective manner. It is from this point of view that the *gramdan* movement deserves almost encouragement".

Gramdan provides opportunity to eradicate the class distinctions of haves and have-nots but creates a sense of service and sacrifice among the people. *Gramdan* provides a method of land distribution by weeding out private ownership of land and giving the land to everyone in the village at a ratio of the requirements of each family based on the number of its members. That every man in the village should receive a plot of land to work upon, is the fundamental idea of *gramdan*. This is to be achieved by doing away with the unequal distribution of land and by avoiding uneconomic holdings and unduly large holdings of land. The method of the land distribution may differ from village to village and each village can adopt its own course. All the land of a village can be pooled into one common plot and distributed to each family for cultivation according to their need and strength to work. Every individual will cease to be the owner of land and the right of ownership will vest in the village community as a whole. The concept of *Gramdan* is a comprehensive one as it envisages to solve so many problems at one and at the same time.

Explaining the significance of *Gramdan*, Vinoba points out five-fold programme of this revolution, (1) Creating an atmosphere of economic equality and liberty. (2) Reviving the cultural life of the society by making the village a family. (3) Discarding the land ownership concept, thus creating ethical atmosphere to settle disputes mutually without litigation, bad blood or bitterness. (4) Establishing old *Varnashrama Dharma* which is derivative of peace, fearlessness, compassion and faith. (5) Protecting the society from outward aggression thus acting as a defense measure.

The salient features of a *gramdan* village can best be summarised as follows (1) Involvement of more people enthusiastically to work for its aims so as to make them proud of their own village. (2) Besides agriculture preference to village crafts is helpful in reducing the burden of population on land. (3) Agricultural production, to begin with, may take the form of owner-cultivation or cooperative farming but ideal to be striven is that of a village communal farming or *gramdan* farming, in which the whole village will work as a joint family. (4) the multicraft and many sided *Sarvodaya* method of production ensures that each village and each family will have to devote itself not only to agriculture but to one or more crafts.

Explaining the significance of *gramdan*, Vinoba enumerated seven basic objectives: (1) Elimination of poverty, (2) Awakening the feelings of affection and love in the hearts of the land-owners; thus improving the moral atmosphere in the country, (3) Strengthening the society by forging bonds of mutual help and fellow-feelings, thus avoiding what is as a rule witnessed elsewhere in the form of class hatred between the land-holders on one side and landless on the other. (4) Revival and furtherance of Indian culture based on our unique philosophy of *yajna, dan* and *tapa*, thus strengthening the faith of man in true religion. (5) Building a new soical order on the basis of voluntary bodily labour, non-possession, co-operation and self-reliance. (6) Giving an opportunity to all the political parties in the country to come together on a common platform and work unitedly, thus rooting out bitterness and self-agrandisement. (7) Helping world peace.

Gramdan has transformed the land gift movement into village gift. Some conditions are to be fulfilled so as to be called as *gramdan* village. They are the following. (1) More than 50 per cent of the total land should be donated by private land owners. (2) Atleast two-third of the adult residents should join the movement. (3) Disputes should not be taken to the police or to the court, but should be settled in the village itself by a special committee setup for the purpose. (4) The members of the village should contribute a portion of the their income as *Gram Kosh* (Community fund) say 1/40 of their agricultural produce for the welfare of the community, with first priority to the weaker sections of the community. (5) There should be a duly constituted *Gram Sabha* and all adults residing in the village should be eligible for membership. (6) Individual owners should be willing to transfer their ownership to the *Gram Sabha* and should allow a minimum of 5 per cent of their lands to be distributed among the landless in the village.

It is an admitted fact that *Bhoodan* and *Gramdan* did not meet with complete success. However Vinoba could effect a change in attitude, which would by itself lead to socio-economic impact. In 1957, he said, "Let it be understood clearly that increasing agricultural production is certainly not the aim and object of *Bhoodan* and *Gramdan*. That would be only incidental. Its main object is to widen man's loyalty to the entire society".[15] Further he said, "I am not really worried about how the work of reconstruction will proceed in the *Gramdan* villages. The task of building up a new society of the free and equal in the *Gramdan* villages is a responsibility which all have to share. It is not our private or personal commitment. I am out to pose problems, not to solve them. I am not a full-stop; I voluntarily give up their private ownership is my task".[16]

Regarding the attitudinal change, both *bhoodan* and *gramdan* envisaged and effected a high degree of result. The movement directly influences the life of the landlords and landless people. By adopting Gandhian ideas, Vinoba could keep the social reconstruction more alive at a period when even the educated people were labelling the Gandhian concepts as irrelevant. It induced interest in the individual to dwell into Gandhian thought and reassess its relevance.

The *Bhoodan* and *Gramdan* movements are not without defects. Too much reliance on the mechanism organisation, lack of faith in land donors, lack of committed *Sarvodaya* workers, too much of focus on some selected areas etc., have resulted in an imbalanced percolation of the ideology and an uneven spread-up of the message contained in it. More rigid approach to the target-oriented policy led to many lacunae and lack of acceptance of the scheme widely. The failure in devising some short-term strategies for the solution of the pressing problems of landless was another defect. Further it failed to influence the government effectively. Thus the spirit of the movement gradually got diluted.

As of now, only 30 per cent of the land have been redistributed. The reasons are as follows: (1) The land donation should be made legal. It is a difficult, tedius and complex phenomenon and takes much time and energy. The disputes of ownership, the donations by ex-rulers, etc. have caused the delay. (2) Though the landlords have made the donations, the intermediary agents have refused to vacate the donated lands. (3) Some landlords after donating the land on the eve of the nation-wide movement, have tried to withdraw the donation after a second thought. (4) A major part of the lands were barren, rocky, undulating, eroded, swampy or otherwise degraded, being unfit for redistribution. (5) The *Sarvodaya* movement lacked resources, manpower and dynamism. The old guards prevented the youths from entering the movements. (6) the *Bhoodan* Boards have acute shortage of financial and human resources.

Some of the suggestions regarding the working of *Bhoodan* movement are as follows. (1) No donation of land should ordinarily be accepted from those villagers who have holdings of less than five acres. (2) Inferior land should be avoided as far as possible. (3) No uncultivable land received in donation should be brought under cultivation. (4) The organisers of the movement should provide necessary inputs and equipment to the landless peasants. (5) Full and detailed records of the donation of the land, livestock and material should be kept. The Sarva Seva Sangh should see that the records are properly maintained. (6) The government should be urged to take up the necessary legislation for just and equitable distribution or redistribution of land cattle and other materials among the landless.

The concept of *Dan* does not apply only to those who have land, wealth or property but also to those who can place their physical labour for service of the community. *Jeevandan* calls for the voluntary acceptance of a simple life and hard work dedicated for the service of others. *Sampatidan* calls for the acceptance of the principle of Trusteeship. Regarding *Jeevandani*, Jayaprakash Narayan said, "A *Jeevandani* is expected to embrace hardship and simplicity, of the land or any other property or income, he is expected to make his due contribution to *Bhoodan* or *Sampatidan*. If he has no independent means of livelihood, he is naturally not expected to live on air. If the inner voice prompts such a person to take the plunge, he should do so unhesitatingly in the faith the great society, whose full time servant he becomes, will not forget him. The movement, needless to say, will not forget him. But he should be prepared for hard work and simple living. He should also be prepared for manual labour".[17]

The concept of Jeevandan puts a sort of moral obligation of the society also to look to the welfare of the person, who dedicates his life in the service of the society. Like *Gramdan* and *Sampatidan, Jeevandan* inculcates the feelings of equality and brotherhood and brings in its wake social welfare. Jayaprakash Narayan said, "Ours is a democracy. We vote a government into power. We are masters of the government. It is, therefore, quite irresponsible on our part to think that; the Prime Minister or the Chief Minister would devise ways and means of solving our problems. The State will carry out its functions, but one should not forget that we too have a duty towards neighbour and the village people."[18]

On 24 October, 1952, at Patna, Vinoba placed his *Sampatidan* idea for the first time. "As the work of *Bhoodan* progressed it became increasingly clear that the idea behind the movement could not be fulfilled, unless we went further and asked for a portion of wealth and property. Hence, I made up my mind that I must also ask for a share of wealth and property from the people. I place my demand at one-sixth of it; but it is up to the people to decide what they could and would give me", remarked Vinoba. On 12, March, 1953, he added *Shramdan*, which means contribution of manual labour. He started breaking some dry land everyday for 15 minutes. This donation was raised by one minute everyday, until he gave an hour for *Shramdan* daily. Village people of all categories joined him in large numbers in this programme.

The Sixth Annual Sarvodaya Sammelan was held in April 1953 at Bodh Gaya. It was at this conference that Jayaprakash Narayan announced his *jeevandan* and resolved to retire from active party politics to devote his whole time to constructive work. Vinoba visited Bengal on 1 January, 1955. By this time, the Avadi Session of the Indian National Congress adopted a resolution on *Bhoodan* and *Sampatidan*. "The Congress warmly welcomes the *Bhoodan* movement started by Vinoba. The *Bhoodan* and *Sampatidan* movement, apart from tackling certain economic problems, is essentially a moral movement for bringing about a socio-economic revolution voluntarily and through peaceful means. The Congress places on record its deep sense of appreciation of the great work done by Vinoba and appeals to all Congressmen to give their fullest cooperation to this movement".

The Seventh Annual Sarvodaya Sammelan was held at Puri in March 1955 and Vinoba remarked the role of *Bhoodan* and *Gramdan* movement in bringing out world peace. He said, "Wherever you go for *Bhoodan*, tell them, that every donation is conducive to world peace. If such a material and inert particle as the atom can be a source of tremendous energy, what a mighty tower of energy can be such a vital, life-containing and knowledge bearing object as man".[19]

Vinoba thought that the *Bhoodan* movement could be an important basic activity for correlating various subjects of study to the physical and social environment of the area. *Bhoodan* touches the problem of land, food and village industries and promotes new values in life. It can serve as a good medium of education for children both in villages and cities. His *Bhoodan* tours have convinced him that Village Panchayats could function equitable only when social and economic disparities have been liquidated in these rural communities. He opines that full-fledged Panchayats should be established only in those villages where land has been redistributed either through *Bhoodan* or legislation, and where village and cottage industries have been established on a co-operative basis.

Vinoba entered Telangana in January 1956. After completing his Andhra tour with a collection of nearly 63,000 acres, he entered Tamil Nadu and declared, "the *Bhoodan* movement is founded on the rock of love and universal brotherhood of man. We should make a start towards our ultimate goal of 'one world' *Jai Jagat*. We must rise above parochial and caste distinctions. *Bhoodan* knows no language except the language of love".

The Eighth Annual Session of the Sarvodaya Sammelan was held at Kancheepuram in the last week of May 1956. On 21 November, 1956 at a meeting in Palani in Madurai District, Vinoba asked the workers to stand on their own feet and discard connections with any fund extending financial assistance to the movement, but to work on people's participation. This decision enthused the local workers to intensify their activities in the villages. As a result, many villages in Madurai District were donated as *Gramdan*.

The Ninth Annual Session of the Sarvodaya Sammelan was held at Kaladi in May 1957. Vinoba explained the importance of *Gramdan*. He said, "*Gramdan* means equitable distribution of *Samyayoga*. But let us remember that equality connot be brought about by hard-heartedness. *Samyayoga* without compassion of heart is futile. *Gramdan* connotes indentification of one and all with the whole. In *Gramdan*, land-holders have to offer their lands, landless workers their labours,. and intellectuals the intellect. Dedication from all elements is the key to *Gramdam*"[20]

A *Gramdan* conference was held at Yelwal on 21 September, 1957. Explaining the basic idea of *Gramdan*, Vinoba said, "In the world today there are in fact no have-nots; some possess land, others property, and yet others intellect and physical labour. Furthermore love and affection permeate the hearts of all human beings. In the *Gramdan*, the landlords should donate land and the working class their labour for the development of the community. *Gramdan* is a total idea. It includes *Khadi* and Village industries, Shanti Sena, Basic education and ultimate establishment of a non-violent social order. It must lead to higher production of food for achieving national self-sufficiency. I, therefore, regard *Gramdan* as a defence measure; there can be no real security for India without achieving self-reliance in food requirement".[21] At a public meeting in Yelwal, Nehru declared that *Gramdan* had come to stay and Namboodripad admitted that the *Gramdan* movement provided an alternative to their own policy in respect of the land problem.

Vinoba entered Gujarat on 22 September, 1958. In his post-prayer meeting at the Vedichi Ashram he stated "welfare state is not socialism, because everything in it depends on state authority. All power and initiative is concentrated in the hands of the state. It depends on the power of the armed forces. There can be no real democracy in a state as long as it depends on its armed strength. If I ever thought of contesting an election my electoral programme will be of 3 points: (1) Disbanding of the armed forces. (2) Abolishing special class of men who are forced to take to scavenging. (3) Banning textile mills. I know no one will vote for me. We have to create a strong public opinion for our programme".

The Eleventh Annual Session of the Sarvodaya Sammelan was held at Ajmer in February 1959. Vinoba highlighted the significance of Shanti Sena. He said, "I regard the Shanti Sena work not only national in character, but truly international. In these days of advanced science, we cannot get at the right step unless we think in international context. That is why our slogan is *Jai Jagat*".

In the beginning of the movement, a village was declared as *Gramdan*, when all the land holders, big and small, surrendered their proprietary rights and transferred their lands to the village community for redistribution among the people according to the size of the families. Experience, however, indicates that such a scheme of *Gramdan* was difficult to implement and the results were, consequently, quite meagre. In consultation with *Sarvodaya* workers, Vinoba, therefore, evolved a simpler pattern called *Sulab Gramdan*, Under it 75 per cent of cultivators in village contribute at least 5 per cent of their lands for redistribution among the landless; 95 per cent of the remaining land would be in their possession for actual cultivation, though its legal ownership has to be transferred to the village community. The land retained by the farmers cannot, howerver, be sold or mortgaged outside the village without the special sanction of the *Gram Sabha*. A Village Development Fund is also created, each family making an annual contribution equivalent to one-thirtieth of the agricultural produce, or one-fourtieth of the total income. Those who do not possess land should contribute proportional free labour for any project decided upon by the community. All adults living in the village constitute the *Gram Sabha* which has to manage the affairs on the principle of unanimity or consensus, and not on the basis of majority decisions. A village is declared as *Gramdan* when atleast 75 per cent of its residents signify their approval in writing to the above-mentioned conditions, including sufficient number of land-owners, so that atleast 51 per cent of the total land belonging to resident owners is covered under *Gramdan*.

Almost all the State Governments have already enacted necessary *Gramdan* legislation to recognise this work and accord it the sanction of authority. But the legal confirmation of *Gramdan* village has proved to be very slow. It involves the use of a large amount of correspondence and in filling up elaborate forms including village statistics. To cite an illustration, out of 8,000 villages in Darbhanga district, only 51 villages have so far been legally confirmed under the Bihar *Gramdan* legislation. Furthermore, sice the workers, after completing *Gramdan* scheme in a district, moved to another district the tempo of follow-up action was naturally very feeble. Experienced *Sarvodaya* workers are also limited in number. While constructive workers secure *Gramdan* villages, it is the duty of the government to organise reconstruction work in those areas. The state is, obviously, expected to cooperate with the movement in a variety of ways and there should be the closest co-ordination between *Gramdan* and Community Development administration.

REFERENCES

1. Jayaprakash Narayan. *Jeevandan*. p. 6.
2. Jayaprakash Narayan. *A Picture of the Sarvodaya Social Order*. p. 30.
3. *Ibid*., p.1.
4. *Ibid*., p. 43.
5. *Ibid*., p.12.
6. Damodardas Mundra, *Bhoodan Gangotri*, p. 42.
7. *Ibid*., p. 99.
8. *Ibid*., p. 104.
9. Nirmala Deshpande, *Bhoodan Ganga*. Vol. 1, pp. 19-20.
10. Damodardas Mundra, *Bhoodan Gangotri*, p. 163.
11. K. S. Bharathi, *The Philosophy of Sarvodaya*. pp. 127-128.
12. *Ibid*., pp. 130-131.
13. Jayaprakash Narayan, *Gramdan and Swaraj*, p. 92.
14. *Ibid*., p. 84.
15. Vinoba, *Gramdan—Why and How*. p. 18.
16. Vinoba, *Bhoodan*. p.1
17. Jayaprakash Narayan, *A Picture of Sarvodaya Social Order*. p. 34.
18. Jayaprakash Narayan. *Gramdan and Gram Swaraj* p. 77
19. K. S. Bharathi, *The Philosophy of Sarvodaya*. p. 148
20. *Ibid*.. p. 149.
21. *Ibid*.

4

ON THIRD POWER

Vinoba delivered a speech at the Sarvodaya Sammelan, Chandil, Singhbhum, Bihar on 9 March, 1953. This has been reproduced here as such:

> "This is a gathering of workers. We have met here to offer to God whatever we have done during the past year and to carry away with us provision for the year ahead. At this juncture we need to give some thought to three things—our methods, our programmes, and the ways in which our work may be integrated.
>
> No matter where we are working or what we are doing the state of the world is such that work cannot be done in isolation from the total world picture. We cannot take the smallest step without being continually aware of the influences at work in the world, the new trends which arise, the interplay of ideas and the conflicts of emotion. It is plain that the world is in a very unsettled state; it is also in a very explosive state. Any thing may happen at any moment. The mental climate, and the outward conditions, are equally unsettled."

A month or two ago a number of intellectuals and learned men met in Delhi and held deliberations on the philosophy of non-violence. Our revered Rajendra Babu in addressing the gathering, said: "No nation in the world today has the courage and confidence to declare that it can govern without an army". He went on to say, sorrowfully: "Even though we had Gandhiji's teaching direct from his own lips, even though we worked side by side with him, India herself today lacks that courage. Our great leader, Pandit Nehru, has said on many occasions that 'Not a single world problem can be solved by force of arms".

These comrades of ours, on whom our country has laid the responsibility of leadership, believe from their hearts in non-violence and have no faith in the efficacy on violence. And yet they have had to assume responsibility for forming, extending and strengthening the army. This is the evil paradox of the situation in which we find ourselves today.

> "We are in the position of putting our faith in one thing while in action we are forced into something else. It is our heart's desire to see non-violence accepted throughout India and the world, so that men no longer fear one another, but live together in love. Our hearts are filled with the faith that only love can endure and that love can overcome every obstacle. At the same time we possess something called the intellect (*buddhi*). Heart and intellect are inextricably intermingled; each is a part of the other. On the one hand, the heart tells us that no problem can be solved by violence, and that even when violence appears to solve one problem, ten new ones will arise in it place. The intellect, however partakes of all three *gunas*; it can be responsive, it can also be dull; it can also be blind. This heterogeneous intellect tells us, 'We cannot get rid of the army. The people whom we represent have neither the strength nor the skill to do without it. As their representatives, therefore, it is our duty to see that an army is organised, expanded and properly equipped".

This is the state of affairs. Our desire to give our energies to some constructive service is a 'heart' desire only, and our intellect intervenes to say: "But the army must be organised efficiently, and that means organising the kind of industry which can maintain it". For those who have no faith in the spinning wheel this poses no problem, but for people like us the question arises whether arms production can be organised on the basis of spinning and other village industries. Their intellect—and ours too, for we cannot stand a side—says: "No; small-scale industries like these cannot provide a base for arms production".

'Community projects' have now been started in some places, and the government wishes to extend their work to all our five hundred thousand villages, so that the problem of poverty may be overcome and the national wealth and prosperity increased. But if world war should break out tomorrow, I doubt whether even one of these projects would survive, and even those who have organised them share my doubt. The intellect would at once take charge, and the heart would be silenced. 'The main thing now', the intellect would assert, is to save the nation'.

I say this in a spirit of self-examination. If we ourselves were to occupy the seats of power and carry the responsibilities our friends now carry, our actions would differ very little from theirs. The seats of power are magic chairs. Those who occupy them are obliged to think in narrow, limited, artificial and conventional way. They are compelled willy-nilly to think in terms of world trends as they appear to be. The trend is to fear. America, Russia and other big countries fear one another. Weaker nations like India and Pakistan also fear one another. And even though we are convinced that none of our problems can be solved by these mutual fears, weapons or armies, we still base our policies on military strength, and the strange thing is that we are helpless to give it up. When a man is driven helplessly into any action, it is no matter for pride, it is a matter for pity. We in India are in that pitiable condition.

Rajendra Babu has reminded us that the people look to the Sarvodaya Samaj to fulfil one task—that of faithfully maintaining its own basic principles, and of creating a congenial atmosphere for these principles to be practised today. If the Sarvodaya Samaj could do this it would be of the greatest assistance to our national government. In fact, if one of us today were to take office, and become involved in all the schemings and stratagems of office, neither his schemes nor his stratagems would be of as much help to the government as the efforts of the man who devotes himself to building up a society free from military force.

People often ask me why I am out of politics and why I do not accept responsibility in the government of the nation. I answer: "Two bullocks have already been yoked to the cart; of what use would it be to take me as a third? The best way for me to help the cart along is to repair the road so that it can travel in the right direction". We must devote ourselves to building up an independent 'people's power' (*lok-shakti*), and that in itself will be our true service both to the government and to the nation.

By 'an independent people's power' I mean a power inhering in the people, which is totally opposed to the power of violence, but other than the power of the law, and which it must be our task to call into being. We have handed over the power of the law to our government, and although it contains an element of coercion, we regard it as being in a different class from out-and-out violence because society as a whole has conferred these legal powers on the government. It is our task to create a situation in the country in which there will be no need to use even these sanctions of the law. If we can do that we shall have fulfilled our own true *dharma*. If, on the other hand, in our greed for results we depend on the power of the law for carrying on our public service, the distinctive work which is expected of us will not be completed, it may even be hindered.

Public service based on legal authority is certainly possible, and for that very reason we in India have sought, and assumed, control of our own government. So long as society needs a government, we must not shirk the responsibility of government. The duties of government are undoubtedly a service to the nation, but they are not the kind of service which can ever make the sanctions of the law unnecessary.

I will illustrate what I mean by an example. Picture a battlefield where soldiers are being wounded. Those who go to the help of the wounded are filled with compassion; they serve friend and for alike at the risk of their own lives, like a mother serving her children. There is no doubt about their human kindness and the value of their service. But they cannot stop war. Their service is bound up with a society which accepts war. One and the same war machine has two parts, one to kill, the other to rescue the wounded. The contrast between these two functions is clear; everyone can see that one is cruel and the other merciful. War is made up of the cruelty of the one and the humanity of the other, and both work together to ensure that war goes on. To speak in the blunt language of science, so long as we accept war at all we are guilty of its crimes, whether we fight or whether we nurse the wounded. I have given this example to show that we must not imagine that we can create a merciful government by a few merciful actions. Government in essence means brute force.

If our works of mercy are subject to the overall authority of the kingdom of brute force and done by order of the unmerciful, we are not doing our real work. On the surface this Government-sponsored work appears humane, even constructive; we may be tempted to take it up by the prospect of quick results, without looking at it in the wider perspective. If so, we shall no doubt achieve something, but we shall not give the service which is our own distinctive responsibility and both we and others regard as our true *dharma*. It is our duty to find means of putting an end to war itself. This does not mean that we should refuse to help the wounded—we should certainly do what we can to care for them—but we should always remember that this is not our real work.

Let me take another example. Everyone says to me: "You seem to carry some weight with the government; why do not you put pressure on it to get legislation to secure land distribution without compensation?" I tell these friends: "I am not blocking legislation; on the contrary, the work I am doing will make legislation much easier, eve though I may not be cent per cent successful, but only 75 per cent or 50 per cent. I am not obstructing legislation, I am facilitating it. I am creating a climate of opinion in its favour". But if I were to go further, if I were to declare and insist that without making laws, nothing can be done, then I should have betrayed my own *dharma*. My *dharma* calls on me to believe that we can evoke such a spirit in the hearts of the people, that without the aid of legislation, and no matter what the law may say, they themselves will distribute the land. Do mothers need a law to induce them to nurse their babies? There is a power in the heart of man which enriches his life, and that power is love. Man depends on love, he is born of love, he is nourished by love and when the time comes for him to leave the world, he dies content if he can see his dear ones around him at the last. If, in spite of this experience of the power of love, we have not the courage to appeal to it in the wider life of society, and go on demanding legislation instead, we shall not be able to help our government in the way it expects of us—by building up 'people's power'. This is our task, to build up a people's power which is distinct from the power of the State. I say that these two powers are distinct; I do not say that they are opposed, or incompatible. What is incompatible with people's power is the power of violence.

Let me cite one more example. The Government wishes to help in the *khadi* programme and has established a Khadi Board. Pandit Nehru expressed his surprise that something which should have been done four years earlier (soon after Independence) had been so long delayed. The Government desires to extend the scope of *khadi* work and increase production. It is our duty, and that of the Charkha Sangh to help the government in this work. The Charkha Sangh has experience in this field, and the assistance of men of experience will be needed. But here again, in my opinion, although we should give the government the help expected of a knowledgeable citizen, we must not become wholly absorbed in its programme; otherwise we shall not be able to carry out our own *khadi* programme properly. We may help the Government as much as we can with production, but at the same time we should be a clear about our own point of view and carry on our own work accordingly. Let us never lose sight of the fact that our *khadi* work is a means to the establishment of a village-centred polity.

Pandit Nehru came to see me and spoke with great affection and I listened humbly to what he had to say. When he asked my advice, I expressed my views briefly. I said: "We expect the government to treat *khadi* and village industries in the same way as it treats the subject of literacy. We accept the principle that every citizen must be able to read and write, because this is an essential part of citizenship. The government therefore recognises an obligation to make everyone literate. Circumstances may make it impossible to succeed completely but so long as we do not succeed, so long as some remain illiterate, our conscience will continue to prick us. Let our government, in the same way, accept the proposition that it is its duty to teach every citizen and villager of India to spin. Let the government accept the idea that a villager or townsman who does not know how to spin is not properly educated. The people will do the rest. We do not ask the government for money. The greatest assistance that they can give us is the acceptance of the idea". Nehru heard me with patience, and I think he liked the proposal. He said half-jokingly: "If everyone is taught to spin, how will the yarn be used?" I countered: "If everyone is to be taught to read, how will the reading be used?" I have met many persons who have had two or three years of schooling but never found any use for it for the rest of their lives. But, as you see, I asked no more for *khadi* than this, that a popular government should be ready to fulfil the desires expressed by its people. It I had gone further, and demanded that *khadi* should be forced upon the people by law, I should have shown myself ignorant of my own duty, and forgotten my own slogan, that we must establish a people's power distinct from the power of law.

I have given illustrations of my theme from *Khadi* and from the *Bhoodan* programme. We have our own method of solving the land problem. If our government, democratic as it is, decides to tackle the problem it will do so by legislative authority. There is nothing wrong in that, it is merely a different way of doing things. But Government help of this kind will not nurture the power of the people, although it may increase their prosperity. Our aim, on the other hand, is not merely that people should be prosperous, it is that they should realise their power. This lies at the root of all our work; if that objective is kept steadily in view, there will be no need to spend much time on discussions of methods. Every constructive activity will be characterised by methods which we may expect to result in an attitude of independence and self-reliance *vis-a-vis* the authority of the government.

If we think along these lines it naturally follows that the two main characteristics of our work will be discipline of thought and a wide sharing of authority.

By 'discipline of thought' I mean that ideas should be clearly understood and expounded. Nothing should be accepted without understanding the principles involved. It should be a matter for regret when anyone accepts our ideas without having understood them; we should be satisfied with explaining our ideas without imposing our will on others. Same people say that the Sarvodaya Samaj is a 'loose organisation'. A loose organisation would certainly be useless and serve no purpose. But the Sarvodaya Samaj is not a loose organisation; it is not an organisation at all. It is a society based solely on ideas. We compel none to carry them out without first understanding them, and we will not obey anyone's orders without first considering and approving them. We meet only to exchange our duties. The *Koran*, in singing the praises of the saints, says that their work is marked by mutual consultation. We too must devote ourselves to mutual consultation and pooling of ideas. We should be happy when people refuse to accept our ideas because they are not convinced; we should be very unhappy if someone puts these ideas into practice without understanding them. It seems to me that there is more strength in such an organisation than in one which is efficient, clear-cut and bound by regulations. I am not saying that a strictly regulated legislative organisation has no power at all; but that its power is not *Shiva-Shakti*, it is not a power for good. It is because we wish to create *Shiva-Shakti* that we desire only the discipline of ideas.

It follows, then, that one aspect of our work is dissemination of ideas. From this point of view I can see why Lord Buddha established the *Bhikshu Sangha* and Shankaracharya the *Yati Sangha*. I have, it is true, come to the conclusion that we ourselves should not form any such *Sangha*, because experience shows that their defects are likely to outweigh their advantages. Nevertheless we ought to reflect on the reasons why those great men felt the need of *Sanghas* and on the ideas that lay behind them. We want our ideas to flow out to people like a perennial spring of water, and therefore, we need messengers to carry them. Without such messengers the Sarvodaya Samaj cannot do its work. We must take every opportunity for meeting people and coming into close touch with them. People are not likely to accept our ideas at the first hearing; our workers must be filled with such enthusiasm that they will enjoy repeated discussions with the same groups, their faith and confidence in the power of the idea must be strong enough for that.

The fact is that many of us have got entangled in various institutions. These institutions have their own importance no doubt. Nevertheless let us show our regard for what they stand for without becoming attached to the institutions as such. Let them continue their work, but let some of their members be always moving about among the people. If we do not organise our work on some such lines, our ideas will lose their vigour, and the discipline of ideas will not be effective.

The Bihar workers say with some pride—and the pride is justified—that it was the Bihar Congress that first took up *Bhoodan*, which was later approved by the All-India Congress at the Hyderabad sitting. But what does this approval amounts to?—A circular from the top, from the All-India office, that "every Congressman must help the *Bhoodan* movement". As the *Ganga* comes down to Haridwar from the Himalaya, so the circular comes down to the State offices. The *Ganga* moves on from Haridwar to its lower reaches; the circular too moves on towards the district offices. No matter how far the *Ganga* flows, it remains nothing but water; and in exactly the same way the circular remains nothing but paper. Like begets like, every species reproduces its own kind, and circulars beget nothing but circulars. Yet the work must be done after all, by the village people themselves. And how is this circular to reach the villages when it simply goes from one office to another?

So the work of the *Bhoodan Yagna* will not be successful unless we reach every home. Our goal is to collect twenty-five lakhs of acres of land from five lakhs of villages. Put like that is seems easy. Five acres per village on an average is not a big thing. But who is to reach every village? Therefore, the most important tool we possess is the dissemination of our ideas; we must plan for it and make our programme accordingly.

But if you are not bold enough for this, if you quail before the prospect of carrying the message to every village, and turn instead to short cuts by proposing legislation, then I must tell you that making laws, and relying on laws, is not our job. By all means let there be laws, good laws, as quickly as possible. But if we get involved in the law making, we shall be forsaking our own calling, our own *dharma*, for an alien vocation. Our own job, our *dharma*, is to travel round the villages and to maintain our faith in our ideas. Do not say that the work will never be done by discussion of ideas. The work will never be done in any other way. It can be done only through acceptance of the idea. The power of the idea, the discipline of the idea, is our first tool.

Our second tool is that of decentralisation of authority. This means that all capacity for work, and all power that accrues from work, should be built up in every village instead of being centralised. To that end, we desire that every village should have the right to decide for itself what things should come into it and what should not. For instance, if a village decides to run a village oil-press and therefore, excludes mill-processed oil, it should have the right to stop mill oil from coming in. When we propose this, the government tells us that it is not possible to have 'a state within a state'; but what we must understand is that unless we distribute power and authority in this manner, military rule is inevitable. We cannot do without the army today, we shall not be able to do so tomorrow. In practice you will have to make up your minds to make use of the army, and therefore to maintain it in good order. In that case, do not pretend that you want ever to be rid of it.

But if we really do desire to rid ourselves of the army, we must do what God has done. God has distributed to each of his creatures a share of intelligence. Everyone has been given his portion, the scorpion, the serpent, the lion and the man. True, some creatures have less and some more; but God gave a share to each one and commanded them to manage their own lives but their own intelligence. The creation has worked so smoothly on this plan that God is able to take complete rest, so much so that men even doubt that He really exists. We should do the same; we should so manage the government that people doubt whether there is a government. If people were to begin saying that India appears to be without a government, you may be sure that the rule of non-violence has begun.

That is why we call for *Gramswaraj*. We want to see the power to manage its own affairs vested in the village, that is in the hands of the villagers. They should for example stand up and decide for themselves what things they will produce, and they should inform the Government what things they wish to exclude. If the Government cannot or will not stop these things coming in the villagers must be bold enough to oppose it. If this kind of people's power is built up it will be a great help to the Government, and will do away with military sanctions; but without it the power of the army will never be ended.

Even if Delhi were to acquire the intellect of the Lord *Brahma*, with four brains, and eyes for all the four points of the compass, it could never plan for, and manage, all the affairs of every village with benefit to them all.

Therefore we should have village planning instead of national planning. I said 'instead of'. It would be far better if 'national planning' really meant 'village planning', and that Delhi should give the villages whatever help they may need in their planning. This is the second part of our programme. Whatever we do is in the direction of decentralisation of authority, and that is why we wish to distribute land in the villages.

When the question of the land is raised, some persons want to prescribe a 'ceiling', a maximum legal holding. This proposal has been put forward ever since the *Bhoodan* movement began to take hold of the people. But I say, first decide the minimum to be given to every one. Why do I say this? It is because I desire to distribute authority. Today the labourers are all working for someone else. They work, but the direction of the work is not in their hands. The wheels of work roll on, but the workers are not responsible. We want them to put into their work not merely their hands and their feet, but their brains and their hearts also. There are some who argue that Indian labourers have such limited intelligence that it is better they should work under the direction of others. But that is not the way of non-violence. What intelligence they possess is our capital; if we let that go, we have no other intelligence to take its place.

Let us admit that a capitalist is often more intelligent than a labourer. But the combined intelligence of all the labourers in the country is equalled by no other intelligence, and our country will be much poorer if it is not put to use. The labourers intelligence whatever it be, must be fully employed. At the same time their mental powers must be stimulated and one method of doing it is to give them land. The gift of land is part of an educational process, it is a tool for developing their intelligence.

Let us now turn our attention to our own movement. We have built up a Sarva Seva Sangh and also a Sarvodaya Samaj. The Sarva Seva Sangh will do the work. It will not be a loose organisation but a strong institution bound by rules. The Sarvodaya Samaj will not be an organisation at all, loose or otherwise. It will be a fellowship of those who believe in the power of the idea. It is our task to strengthen further its basis of ideas. We do not want to create merely a more disciplined group; we must work to make it more fruitful of ideas and more ready to accept ideas as the basis of living. We must work for the creation of a fellowship of ideas among all members of the *Samaj*, whether they are present today or not, whether their names are listed or not. One way of doing this is to be moving about continually, as I have already described, to disseminate our ideas. Another way is to publicise Sarvodaya literature and encourage study, reflection and discussion of it. For this purpose there should be study groups which should make a comparative study of our ideas and those of other ideologies.

We shall next take up a discussion of the programmes we have in hand in the Sarva Seva Sangh.

We have commenced the work of *Bhoodan-Yagna*. In regard to that, my aim and object is that five crore acres of land should change hands. We can do it; we can solve the land problem, if we all work for it . By 'all' I do not mean only you and me, only the Sarvodaya Samaj; I mean all who accept the idea, Congressman, socialists and all others. We may be a 100 per cent successful without legislation, or we may be only 75 per cent or 50 per cent successful, and the law will complete the task. I cannot say exactly what will happen; I am no prophet. But however it happens, it will have to be done mainly by the power of the people. It should be done wholly by them I should dance for joy; but I should be well content if it is done mainly by them. If it can be done, the next election will not set one good man against another in opposing parties, which happens today as it did when Bhishma fought Arjuna. We want no more contests between Bhishma and Arjuna, we want Rama to fight Ravana. A programme which can win the whole hearted devotion of all goodmen will put an end to their present differences. *Bhoodan Yagna* is such a basic programme.

I have started another programme along with this, which I call *Sampattidan Yagna.* Without it, the *Bhoodan* movement cannot succeed, and our programme of economic freedom and equality will not be fulfilled. The programme was in my mind from the beginning, but I had to do one thing at a time; besides, money is not so fundamental a thing as land. So I preferred to take up the land problem, in the light of divine hand in Telangana. Later, when there began to be talk of a complete solution of the land problem in Bihar, I realised that it was possible only if the two movements were carried on side by side. But I am not going to handle that money. Here too authority must be dispersed. Those who offer us money will dispose of it themselves in accordance with our directive.

In addition to the above two, we have a third programme, namely offering of hanks of hand-spun yarn. This is a very powerful thing but we have not realised its power. Let us make this offering in memory of Gandhiji, and as a token of our belief in manual labour, and as a sign that we accept our responsibility for adding to the nation's wealth. I consider it a vote for Sarvodaya. It is a big thing. The only difficulty is that we have to collect it from door to door, in village after village. And that, in my opinion, is not a difficulty but an inspiration, because it gives us a chance to visit every home. We should expand this programme, and aim at a target in terms of lakhs, as we do for land. It will be most helpful in increasing faith in bodily labour.

I want to add one more thing. All the institutions we have established so far have been run on money wealthy people, good people, our friends and well-wishers, have helped us and we have accepted their help. There was nothing wrong in that. But now times have changed, now is the age of labour, and faith in labour must be instilled. Let us then establish a few institutions in each State, founded on manual work, and accepting no gifts except gifts of manual labour. My idea is that vigorous workers could be trained there who could both disseminate our ideas and carry on practical work.

One word more, before I close. This work of ours is not of a sectarian nature. We should not even call ourselves the Sarvodaya group because that also gives a wrong impression. Let us think of ourselves as human beings and nothing else. Otherwise even this Sarvodaya Samaj, with all its freedom from institutionalism, will little by little become a sect, a narrow group in which we shall be separated from others. Let us never allow our tongues to slip into labelling people as 'socialist', 'Congresswala' or 'Sarvodayawala'. Such terms will, of course, continue to be used, because there are men who wish to work under party names and find them useful. But we belong to no party; we are 'the third power'. In the vocabulary of world politics the 'third power' consists of those who are not attached either to the American or to the Russian block. But in my vocabulary, the third power is that power which is opposed to the power of violence, and distinct from the power of the State. There are three kinds of power: first, that of violence; second, that of law; third, our kind of power which is neither the one nor the other. This third power is inherent in man as man, and we seek to realise it on the widest possible scale. And therefore it is not for us to form a separate sect; it is for us to identify ourselves with the common run of humanity and to work among men simply as fellow human beings.

5

ON SWARAJ SASTRA

The principles of self-government were originally conceived in Nagpur Jail. Government is one thing; self-government is another. Government can be had through violence. Self-government is impossible without non-violence. So the thoughtful do not want government but urge people to strive for self-government. *Swarajya* is a term in Vedic language. It is the government of each by each. The science of self-government is ever-growing. Its systems are ever-changing according to time and place. But its fundamental principles are eternal.

Politics may be defined as a science dealing with the organisation or arrangements between themselves of a group or groups of people. Today human society is divided into three classes—upper, middle and lower and politics is then thought to be concerned with the problem of bringing about some adjustment between these three classes. In Hindu society, people are divided into castes in accordance with their occupations, and politics is regarded as concerned with establishing as adjustment between these castes. Some people in this world have too much wealth while others have little or none. It is supposed that there are two classes of people, namely the rich and the poor, and politics is thought of as concerned with the task of establishing some adjustment between these two classes.

Differences in language or religion also give rise to political problems. There are no natural classes in human society. There are only individuals who are less or more capable. There will be three natural forms of administration: (1) A wise or capable individual may administer for all; (2) More than one wise or capable individuals may join together to administer for all; and (3) All the people may combine and equally share in the responsibility of carrying on their own administration. We may call these three types 'rule by one', 'rule by more than one', and 'rule by all'. Rule by one and rule by all represent the two extremes, and therefore they can be of one form only. But rule by more than one can give rise to several forms. It has two natural divisions—rule by the few and rule by the many.

The following should be regarded as elements common under all conditions to all theories and forms of government and administrations:[1]

(a) Aim to serve life—May find expression in reality or only in outward appearance; may conduce to life for all time or at any rate for the time being may serve life in all places or only locally.
(b) Cooperation of the people—May be given voluntarily; or may be obtained by force when the cooperation may be either complete or just sufficient to carry on the administration.
(c) Administration by capable individuals—Who may be either elected or nominated, or who have on their own initiative banded themselves for the purpose.
(d) With one individual as the final authority—who may be appointed by all, or by the many, or by the few or who may be self-appointed.

The following are some of the principles in the light of which forms of government may be tested:[2]

(a) International brotherhood;
(b) Co-operation of all the elements of a nation, a cooperation given with full knowledge, to the best of one's ability, spontaneous and springing from one's heart;
(c) Unity of interests as between the capable few and the masses in general;
(d) Regard for all-sided and equal development of every member of society;
(e) The most extensive distribution of governmental power;
(f) The least amount of governing;
(g) The simplest governmental machinery;
(h) The lowest administrative expenditure;
(i) The smallest organisation for defence;
(j) Spread of knowledge everywhere uninterrupted, and unbiased, or free in the sense of not being forced into teaching only on approved lines.

The best government is one which does not insist on any particular form, but goes on changing its form from time to time. A system of government is not like a principle on which life can be based and which admits of no variations. When people are tired of a particular system they are often on the look out for a new system, but do not take into account the advantages or disadvantages which arise from its special merits or defects. The form of government where everyone will administer the affairs of all will depend on the stage of development of society. But in any form of faultless government the following four characteristics must be found without fail:[3]

(1) Capable individuals will direct their capacity to service of the people.
(2) The people will be fully self-independent and cooperate with each other.
(3) Non-violence will be the basis of their continual cooperation, and of occasional non-cooperation or resistance.
(4) Honest work on the part of any one will be considered to be of equal value.

By capable is meant, the physically stronger and more intelligent. The difference is physiological and at present there is no way of getting over such differences. Public opinion should regard a capable individual who will not use his powers thus for the welfare of society as an offender, judged in the light of the rules of the State. When once public opinion has been formed in regard to this matter, law can be enacted if necessary to enforce it. Control by law or restraint has a place in a non-violent state conducted on the basis of public opinion. Those who pay no heed top the law should be put in the charge of those who have no need for the law, and the rest of society should go on according to law.

Today public opinion has no respect for a thief. The same should be its attitude to the miser or the hoarder. That is, just as a thief is liable to be brought under the law, so public opinion should regard a miser as actionable under the law. In vain it is said that the wealth of the rich should be forcibly taken away from them. Actually the rich do not desire to keep wealth merely for the sake of accumulating it. They do it in order to obtain status, happiness, security for the future, maintenance of children, and fame as benefactors—if not for all of these purposes at least for some of them. The glory of attractiveness that attaches to the capacity of capable individuals lies in nothing else than in service of the people. In such service also lies human contentment. Every individual should earn to the best of his ability. Whoever fails in spite of being able to do so has no right to wealth. At the same time it is true that whoever works to the best of his ability is entitled to an equal share in the collective earnings.[4]

The State exists merely to apply to the whole of society the economic principle which is found everywhere to a greater or less extent in the family. This is a task beyond the powers of the family. If the State does not do this service, there is no need for its existence. The authority of the State must vest in capable individuals, but that authority must be only the authority to serve the people.

Every village should from the economic point of view become for the most part a self-sufficient unit. Conditions should be such that capable individuals will of their own free will help the masses, and the masses also will of their own accord give their cooperation to the capable few. This can happen only the people stand on their own legs. There is no other way. All those needs which we call the primary requirements of life as well as most of what we call secondary requirements should be met by the people of the village from the village itself.

According to the socialist's plan, wealth in first accumulated in one place and then equally distributed. But this involves three dangers. Firstly, as compared with the unitary process of equally and naturally distributing wealth through the very act of production, it increases cost from the economic point of view, as it requires two processes, viz., of first collecting wealth in one place and then of distributing it equally. Secondly, special arrangements have to be made for protecting this collected wealth, and even then it is an easy target for foreign attack. Thirdly, because of all this, the organisation of society becomes so complicated, intricate and its part interdependent that there can be no certainty that the whole mechanism will not some day collapse because of too much friction.[5]

All plans to gather wealth together and then to distribute it entail much strain on the State, and in the end involve also resorting to violence. So if we wish to avoid complicating the organisation of society, placing too much of a strain on the State, and resorting to violence, it is necessary to see that every villager is his own ruler, and that the cooperation between villages is strong like that of fibres of a well-knit rope. When this happens the villager in combination with his village will form a natural and will-nigh self-sufficient political unit.

As essential characteristic of the best state is so to plan that as a rule only good men will be invariably chosen for administering it. But in spite of it there is bound to be a greater or less extent the good or bad effect of the personality of individuals on the administration. The science of political organisation, or the science of Politics in short, is not a regular science like Applied Mathematics, much less like Pure Mathematics. Pure Mathematics moves in the realm of abstract thought, Applied Mathematics in the realm of matter. But the field of politics is in the realm of human affairs, which is different from the realms of abstract thought and matter.

The aim of Politics is to safeguard the entire good of all men, in every form and in such a way as not to produce conflict. For this purpose, (1) the widest franchise, (2) rule according to the opinion of the majority, (3) complete protection of and utmost satisfaction to minorities, (4) freedom to propagate one's opinions, (5) impartial, cheap and easy administration of justice, (6) provision for universal education, (7) code of reformatory punishment, and such like, which are regarded as the external characteristic of a good government, are proper. But owing to Politics being dependent on the human factor, many defects, controversies and disputes are capable of arising, and to get over them, the people should know the right time for cooperation, non-cooperation and resistance have the ability to put them into action as required by circumstances.[6]

Every member of the general public must feel that law is made by the majority opinion of the people, that the people can therefore change it, that so long as they do not change it, and it is not opposed to morality, he should obey it voluntarily, joyfully and unreservedly, even if as an individual he does not like it. Non-cooperation and resistance are two stages of one and the same thing. As compared with the former, the latter is more drastic. Where it is possible by non-cooperation to accomplish what is desired, resistance should not be resorted to. In non-cooperation, the hand of cooperation is withdrawn and an opportunity is given to the opponent for remedying the situation. When it is clear that this much is not enough it becomes necessary to break the law of the State. Non-cooperation and resistance occupy a permanent place in social life. For they are required not only in the political field but also more or less constantly in social relationships, family affairs and in dealings between one individual and another.

In the ideal State, the method of estimating the value of labour cannot be purely mechanical and irresponsible as it is today. The ideal State will feel responsible for maintaining and protecting all its members.

whatever their physical strength, intellectual capacity, or fitness or lack of fitness for work. All cannot work in the same way. Besides, there is also undoubtedly a difference between physical and mental work. In reality it is wrong to speak of economic value of physical or mental service, for service belongs to the moral sphere, and therefore its value can be appraised only in terms of morality. Every individual will receive absolutely equal protection. But that does not mean that he will receive equal wages or salary, for equal wages do not result in equal protection. A man should be given only that much wage as is necessary to fulfil the State's responsibility to give him equal protection.[7]

In short, all the principles mentioned above may be listed as follows:

(1) Every one will receive equal protection.
(2) Service from each will be according to his ability and may therefore be unequal.
(3) To obtain equal protection is not the same as receiving equal wages.
(4) But the inequality which prevails in wages today will under no circumstances exist.
(5) Wages will be as little unequal as possible, or to put it positively will be commensurate.
(6) Inequality in wages will not be in proportion to inequality of service but in proportion to inequality of need.
(7) The total amount of service rendered by all the individuals and the total amount of protection given to them by the State will be equal to each other.

The spirit of service, self-reliance, non-violent strength, and commensurate wages for all these are the four pillars on which the edifice of the State should rest. The outer form of a State may be different according to conditions prevailing in a particular place or time and according to the mental level of society. A family which consists of parents and infants is of a particular form, a family, which consists of parents and boys and girls is of another form, and a family which consists of quite old parents and grown-up sons and daughters is of still another form. Similarly, owing to differences arising from natural causes or due to accidental circumstances, families may be said to be large or small collective or single, and so on. In all these families, the root idea of the family is one and the same, and only the outer form is different.[8]

The hold of violence on our minds is so great than even though violence has failed a thousand times we still continue to put faith on its capacity to succeed. The negative evidence provided by the fact that no State based on violence has survived should suffice to make us conclude that a State cannot survive except through non-violence. It is considered that States which have been able to endure or are still enduring, to a greater or less extent on violence, are anxious to obtain the support of public opinion or in other words of non-violence, a strong suspicion must arise in the minds of even the most confirmed believers in violence that somehow or other non-violence alone provides the basis for making a government endure.

After dismissing the method of violence from our thoughts, we are left only with the method of non-violence. There is no room then for entertaining doubts and suspicions in regard to non-violence. It remains now only to experiment with it in full faith. The principle of outdoing the opponent does not come in the way of non-violence. One man's victory is another man's defeat is true in the realm of violence. In the sphere of non-violence on man's victory is also another man's victory.

When we ware confronted with the problem of choosing between the alternatives of either a non-violent State or preparations for a total war, the way of non-violence does at once attract us; but even then there is need for organisation, training, etc. if we are to have a non-violent State. Though the organisation required for non-violence may be different from that required for a total war, it will have to be so extensive as to touch the life of every individual. We have suggested a plan for this alone. Before it is put into practice it is necessary to educate public opinion which has of itself turned towards non-violence into becoming non-violent with full knowledge. The masses always incline towards non-violence, but they should be made non-violent because of a knowledge of the principles underlying it. For inactive non-violence will not do. Instead there will be need for active non-violence, non-violence which extends to every sphere of life. Non-violence is a faith or outlook relating to all things. Outlook cannot be restricted to one matter only but ought to extend to every aspect of life.[9]

The battle of non-violence does not take place on the battlefield but in the heart. But in non-violence also, there must be preparedness for battle. Even if non-violence spreads throughout the world, there would be need for preparedness. Neither violence nor non-violence allows room for a man to earn all at one time and to enjoy for the rest of his life. It will always be necessary to keep awake the power of resistance. A life of non-violence means not merely occasional sacrifice but perpetual sacrifice, and not merely sacrifice but joy in sacrifice.

According to the non-violent way of thinking, human society is one, and in it separate nations are conceived of merely for the sake of convenience. If a particular nation has the good sense to adopt non-violence, it will not regard itself as separate from and as opposed to the others. It will be anxious to safeguard the legitimate interests of neighbouring nations as those of its own. Certainly whole nations do not become violent and even if they adopt violence, rather it must be said that they adopt violence only because of mutual rivalry. People do not like violence for its own sake. So if a nation appears, which entertains the desire to conduct its affairs in accordance with non-violence, and therefore strives to relate itself to the rest of the world on the basis of non-opposition, it will awaken the conscience of neighbouring nations, make their conscience operate, and to that extent put those nations on the way of non-violence.

A non-violent nation will not dump its goods on another nation by force. In a non-violent nation, every village will be devoted to labour and be self-dependent. Therefore there will be no scope in it for the greed of other nations. If another nation considers the non-violent nations to be opposed to its own interests, then the non-violent nation will in a friendly manner assist that nation to find a way out and to give it entire satisfaction.

A non-violent order implies the existence of public spirited workers who will from day-to-day serve the people in their neighbourhood and be in intimate touch with them all. If everywhere there is a band of such workers, it would be quite easy, in case of a riot breaking out in one place, to quell it with readiness on their part for a little sacrifice. When the rioters see that those who have been serving them and who are their brothers well-known to them are ready to die opposing them, and when they find that they are assured that no harm will befall them and that all their grievances will be readily heard they will be easily quietened.

In the early stages it was unrestrained violence that held the field. Gradually man learnt to curb and limit his violence and the institution called the State came into existence. The formation of the State did not limit violence up to a degree. The advent of the apparatus of government created a new kind of law and order. Even the Vedas have said that the coercive power of the State is the personification of *Dharma*. But gradually the State grew stronger, became more and more powerful till it became all-powerful with the power of destroying the whole world with its military might based on nuclear weapons.

Never in human history had man been so overpowered by fear as he is today. The hydrogen bomb is the symbol of scientific progress and human servitude. Man is wondering how be could limit and tame the power of violence based on nuclear weapons. They are talking of putting a stop to the production of atomic missiles and weapons, destroying those that are already in existence.

It is an illusion to hope to limit or restrict or regulate the power of violence of the modern State. The only rational and sensible alternative is to understand that humanity can exist only when it discards violent weapons and accepts the ideal of building up a society in which there is no coercive State.

Vinoba declared that his aim was the establishment of *Gram Swarajya* which alone could free India's villages from slavery of the colonial system and exploitation by centralised economy. This was opposed to the official policy favouring the establishment of a welfare State. He stood for village ownership of land. This was distinctly different from private ownership in capitalism and State ownership in communism. Vinoba's was the third way to national regeneration and reconstruction.

The basic structure at the village level would consist of (a) a village assembly of all adults, men and woman, which would regulate and develop village life and function autonomously; (b) a village fund; and (c) a village peace corps. This was a structure based entirely on people's power expressing itself in the form of village power. Thus the village would emerge as an organised unit to look after its internal administration, development, and agro-industrial economy. This was a model for democracy at the grassroots based on direct participation by the people.

Vinoba made the concept of self-rule at the village-level clear beyond doubt. He called his movement *Gramdan* which meant that each one was to contribute to his village. No more was the 'Proletariat' the sole vanguard of revolution and no more was its dictatorship necessary. What was required for social revolution was social non-violence. There was the village assembly and the *Shanti Sena*, with the weapon of *satyagraha*, to take care of those opposed to the collective interests of the village and its *Swarajya*.

The ideal envisaged in a *sarvodaya* social order is stateless society. Vinoba wants the state to be abolished. He said, "The *Puran wallahas* are *bhoot satyayugwadis* (believers in the State-free society of the past);

the Communists are *bhavishya satyayugwadis* (believers in the State-free society of the future); while we are *vartaman satyayugwadis* (soldiers trying to build a State-free society in the present)".[10] He presents his views on State more succinctly. He said, "Ethics and politics remain apart and follow different paths. That is why, I am out to establish a *pragya* as opposed to *rajya*; that is, I want a State where there is no government and people govern themselves".[11]

The *sarvodayaites* do not regard the State as an organ of class rule, but an institution standing above society in which a few individuals are saddled in power and thereby exercise political authority. Owing to their lack of knowledge of historical development, they ignore the sociological truth, that, as Engels said, the "State is by no means a power imposed on society from above". This lack of sociological sense leads them to the conclusion that it is the State that concentrates power in the hands of a few individuals.

The *sarvodayaites* reject all parties. Vinoba said, "I do not recognise parties at all. Moreover my study of history, experience of current affairs and thinking, all lead me to the conclusion that parties in our country can, not only, not do much but are in the long run likely to prove disastrous. Service of our fellow beings must be our sole objective".[12] He did not recognise the vital difference between parties of the capitalist class and parties of the working class.

Vinoba had strong objections to elections also. He said, "Political parties and methods of elections bring the new differences which do not allow the servants of society to come together even for a good mission and serve the country which is weak and poor. Elections, a western import, has broken as under every village and torn it into pieces."[13] He took his stand against parliamentary government and rule by majority. In the ideal *sarvodaya* society, decision will not be taken by counting of votes but by general consensus of opinion.

Decentralisation and devolution of economic and political power are the keynotes of the transition to *sarvodaya* social order. A society based on minimum exchange, small peasant production in the rural sector, minimum use of large-scale industry and maximum regional self-sufficiency can only impede the progress of technological advance and thereby human productivity. The ideal "from each according to his capacity to each according to his needs" is unrealisable in a society where human productivity has not registered tremendous rise. The ideal can only be realised if the reign of plenty is established which can satisfy all the wants of the people.

Sarvodaya rightly demands the ending of the present concentration of economic power. But identification of concentration of economic power with large-scale industry is not correct. They tend to overlook the fact that the technical basis of modern industry is revolutionary. The size of the industrial unit does not cause concentration of economic power and the concentration is caused by private ownership of social means of production. The socialisation of means of production can only put an end to this atrocious concentration.

REFERENCES

1. Vinoba, *Swaraj Sastra*, p. 28.
2. *Ibid.*, p. 31.
3. *Ibid.*, pp. 38-39.
4. *Ibid.*, pp. 41-45.
5. *Ibid.*, pp. 48-49.
6. *Ibid.*, pp. 51-52.
7. *Ibid.*, pp. 59-62.
8. *Ibid.*, pp. 66-67.
9. *Ibid.*, p. 72.
10. Suresh Ram, *Vinoba and His Mission*, pp. 189-90.
11. *Ibid.*, p. 166.
12. *Ibid.*, p. 235.
13. *Ibid.*, p. 151.

BIBLIOGRAPHY

Books

Bhave, Vinoba, *Talks on the Gita*, Sarva Seva Sangh, Varanasi.

Bhave, Vinoba, *The Essence of the Quran*, Sarva Seva Sangh, Varanasi.

Bhave, Vinoba, *Democratic Values*, Sarva Seva Sangh, Varanasi.

Bhave, Vinoba, *Swaraj Sastra*, Sarva Seva Sangh, Varanasi.

Bhave, Vinoba, *Shanti Sena*, Sarva Seva Sangh, Varanasi.

Bhave, Vinoba, *The Third Power*, Sarva Seva Sangh, Varanasi.

Bhave, Vinoba, *Sampatti-Dan*, Sarva Seva Sangh, Varanasi.

Bhave, Vinoba, *From Bhoodan to Gramdan*, Sarvodaya Prachuralaya, Tanjore.

Bhave, Vinoba, *Bhoodan Yajna*, Navajeevan Publishing House, Ahmedabad.

Bhave, Vinoba, *Sarvodaya and Communism*, Sarvodaya Prachuralaya, Tanjore.

Bhave, Vinoba, *Gram Swaraj: Our Birthright*, Sarvodaya Prachuralaya, Tanjore.

Bhave, Vinoba, *Science and Self-Knowledge*, Sarva Seva Sangh, Varanasi.

Bhave, Vinoba, *Gramdan*, Sarvodaya Prachuralaya, Tanjore.

Bhave, Vinoba, *Revolutionary Sarvodaya*, Bharatiya Vidya Bhavan, Bombay.

Bhave, A.V., *Anecdotes of Saint Vinoba*, Sarva Seva Sangh, Varanasi.

Bharathi, K.S., *Thoughts of Gandhi and Vinoba*, Concept Publishing Co., New Delhi.

Bharathi, K.S., *The Philosophy of Sarvodaya*, Indus Publishing House, New Delhi.

Desai, N., *Shanti Sena in India*, Sarva Seva Sangh, Varanasi.

Doctor, Adi, H., *Sarvodaya—A Political and Economic Study*, Asia Publishing House, Bombay.

Gandhi, M.K., *Sarvodaya—Its Principle and Programme*, Navajivan Publishing House, Ahmedabad.

Groom, D., *With Vinoba,* Sarva Seva Sangh, Varanasi .

Jaju, S., *The Philosophy of Sampattidan*, Sarvodaya Prachuralaya, Tanjore.

Kripalani, J.B., *Sarvodaya and Democracy*, Sarvodaya Prachuralaya, Tanjore.

Lanza, D.V., *Gandhi to Vinoba—The New Pilgrimage*, Rider and Co., London.

Misra, B.R., *V. For Vinoba—The Economics of the Bhoodan Movement*, Orient Longmans, Delhi.

Narayan, S., *One Week with Vinoba*, A.I.C.C., New Delhi.

Narayan, J., *From Socialism to Sarvodaya*, Sarva Seva Sangh, Varanasi .

Nargolkar, V., *The Creed of Saint Vinoba*, Bharatiya Vidya Bhavan, Bombay.

Ram, S., *Vinoba and His Mission*, Sarva Seva Sangh, Varanasi.

Shah, K., *Vinoba—Life and Mission*, Sarva Seva Sangh, Varanasi.

Sharma, J.S., *Bhoodan and Vinoba—Bibliography*, Indian National Congress, Bombay.

Tandon, P.D., *Vinoba Bhave—The Man and His Mission*, Vora and Co. Bombay.

Tandon, V., *Sarvodaya After Gandhi*, Sarva Seva Sangh Varanasi.

Tandon, V., *Selections From Vinoba*, Sarva Seva Sangh, Varanasi.

Thacker, V., *The Philosophy of Land-Gift Mission*, Sarvodaya Prachuralaya, Tanjore.

Zinkin, T., *Bhoodan or Land Through Love*, Department of Information and Public Relations, Government of Hyderabad.

Magazines and Journals

Bhoodan.
Bhoodan Yajna.
Gandhi Marg.
Harijan.
Khadi Jagat.
Khadi World.
Maitri.
People's Action.
Sarvodaya.

INDEX